I can't wait to show you around St— one day and eat un— we BURST

diddles x

AUSTRALIA COOKS

Aus

ralia

ooks

EDITED BY KELLI BRETT

Contents

Introduction	6
FROM THE EARTH	10
FROM THE SEA	64
FROM THE LAND	124
SOMETHING SWEET	210
Acknowledgements	266
About the editor	267
Index	268

Introduction

Food has always been about family and friends. But now, for many of us, it is also about lifestyle and self-expression. It's about who we want to be and how we want to be perceived.

Once upon a time, no matter what region we lived in, we all ate the same bland food. If you didn't enjoy the basic meat and three veg, you were simply un-Australian. The native foods that our Indigenous tribes have cooked with for over 40,000 years were largely ignored by the wider populace. Early immigrants warned their families that this was not a place where you could buy 'civilised' foods, and encouraged relatives to come armed with spices and canned goods.

Even thinking back to my own childhood in the 1960s and '70s, if you wanted lettuce, it was iceberg or nothing. Nowadays the old iceberg has to compete with cos, coral, butter, oak, endive and red mignonette, not to mention watercress, witlof, sorrel, radicchio, rocket and chard … However, I do hasten to mention that the iceberg is still a strong contender in the 'great Aussie lettuce' stakes. A good prawn cocktail will never go uncelebrated!

I produced and presented 'The Main Ingredient with Kelli Brett' for over 10 years, stimulating food conversations around the globe and across many deliciously diverse topics. Regionality and seasonality have always been important parts of these conversations. It's clear there's a story to be told about our blossoming regional food culture. Today, a trip through most country towns offers the opportunity to travel via your tastebuds. Our food growers, producers and artisans supply us with everything from the most delicious dairy, meat and seafood, to specialty ingredients such as saffron, black garlic and truffles, along with grains, honeys, nuts, olive oils and wines that are now sought out by foodies across the globe. And each and every one of these ingredients has a passionate and talented (and usually a little bit crazy) group of people behind it, dedicated to producing something that contributes to a food culture that we can be proud of.

But what do everyday Australians cook? Do we even cook any more? Let's face it, it's hard to get anything substantial plated up during the commercial breaks on *Masterchef* or *My Kitchen Rules*. The desire to find an answer to these questions, and to connect our communities with our regional food producers, inspired me to create *Australia Cooks*, a cookbook that celebrates those three crucial ingredients — people, place and produce — that make our food culture unique.

ABC Local Radio, with its 52 stations spread across the country, was in a prime position to make a national call-out to foodies to design a dish that defined their region on a plate. With a multitude of flavours to play with, and no shortage of committed food producers and provedores to give them inspiration, we received over 300 original recipes. And with the recipes came inspirational stories of people passionate about their local produce and excited to share it with the rest of Australia. We judged our entries on regionality and balance of flavours. It was tough to narrow it down, but as we were going through the entries, one thing became very clear. Do Australians still cook? Hell yes!

We've included additional recipes from regionally based professional chefs who have built their businesses on championing local ingredients and supporting their food communities. All in all, this beautiful book has been a massive collaboration between hundreds of content makers across ABC Local, as well as chefs, food producers and home cooks across the nation.

The making of this book has left us in no doubt that Australians are wanting to know the stories behind the food that they eat. The recipes in this book have an emphasis on fresh flavours and simplicity; some are a little more indulgent, but they are all delicious and truly demonstrate that we are a nation that loves to cook. I hope you will continue this conversation and that this book will give you lots of inspiration …

From the Earth

From the rich, fertile soils all across this great land comes an abundance of beautiful crops. Celebrate the produce of your region with these gorgeous vegie recipes — not just side dishes, but stars in their own right.

When planning meals, most of us start with the protein and then think about the vegetables almost as an afterthought. But chef Matt Wilkinson, author of *Mr Wilkinson's Favourite Vegetables*, says we've got it all backwards, and that fresh produce should never play second fiddle. He says there's no better way to find out what's in season than by looking at the often cheapest fruits and vegetables. Imagine that? How old-fashioned.

There also seems to be a shift in our perception that only perfect produce can make it onto our plates. Simon Bryant, from ABC TV's *The Cook and the Chef*, has led the pack of Aussie chefs who have a passion for good food that is thoughtfully produced, carefully sourced and respectfully cooked. When Simon told me years ago about his love for ugly fruits and vegetables — those poor crooked carrots and not-so-perfect apples — I thought it would never catch on. But now we're starting to see the light and realise that aesthetic perfection does not necessarily equal good flavour!

When selecting your fruit and veg, think first about what's in season. Seasonal means two great things: it's less expensive and it tastes better! Once you have decided what fabulous seasonal ingredients to make the most of, you can always add some protein if you really feel the need. But with so many delicious vegetarian recipes to choose from, such as Baked pumpkin, Vegetarian savoury lupin pancakes and Upside-down ratatouille, who needs meat?

SALTBUSH RUB

We love this rub because we grow all the main ingredients here in Quorn during the year and dry them for storage. Old man saltbush (*Atriplex nummularia*) is an important native plant in the Flinders Ranges and northern South Australia, and it's a great addition to savoury recipes. In the Flinders, we have access to wonderfully succulent saltbush lamb, delicious roo and rangeland goat — all of which are lovely roasted with this rub. It's also great on grilled fish from the Spencer Gulf, sprinkled over roasted root vegetables, or used like a dukkah with crusty bread and beautiful Flinders Ranges olive oil.

Andrea Tschirner, Quorn, South Australia

MAKES 2 CUPS

1 cup mixed almonds, and pistachios or macadamias
2 teaspoons coriander seeds
1 cup loosely packed dried saltbush leaves (see note)
¾ cup dried herbs (whatever you have on hand, such as parsley, oregano, chives)
sea salt flakes and freshly ground black pepper, to taste

Preheat the oven to 180°C. Gently roast the nuts and coriander seeds on a baking tray until golden and aromatic. (Alternatively, dry-fry in a frying pan over low heat.) Set aside to cool.

Place the cooled nuts and coriander seeds in a food processor. Add the saltbush leaves and herbs, season to taste, and blitz until you have a crumb-like texture.

Store in a glass jar, zip-lock bag or other airtight container and use within 2–4 weeks.

Note: Saltbush can be found across coastal and inland areas of eastern and southern Australia.

SAUTÉED CHESTNUTS

North-east Victoria is the principal growing area in Australia for chestnuts, an autumnal and winter treat. As locals, with three trees of our own, we have mastered the art of peeling this nutritious nut. We like the De Coppi Marone variety as they are easier to peel. We store the nuts in a paper bag in the crisper before peeling, then freeze the peeled nuts in plastic bags in 250 g lots, ready to be used in savoury and sweet recipes. In this recipe, the sautéed chestnuts are perfectly paired with freshly pressed extra-virgin olive oil from the nearby farm gates and farmers' markets, as well as Murray River Gourmet Chilli Salt Flakes.

Joan Simms, Beechworth, Victoria

SERVES 4–6

500 g chestnuts (250 g peeled)
2 teaspoons extra-virgin olive oil
chilli-infused salt

To peel the chestnuts, make a small cut across one side, taking care not to cut too deeply (a Stanley knife is a good tool for this). Place 8–10 nuts at a time in a microwave dish with a lid, add enough water to just cover the nuts and microwave, covered, on high for 4–5 minutes. Place the nuts immediately in a tea towel to sweat and cool. Squeeze the ends to make the cut 'smile' and peel away the skin and membrane. Cut any large nuts in half.

Heat the oil in a small frying pan over low heat. Cook the chestnuts gently for about 5 minutes, or until they are a light golden colour. Drain on paper towel and toss in a bowl with the chilli-infused salt. Serve warm as a snack with drinks.

WATTLESEED OR BUSH TOMATO DAMPER ROLLS

I love enhancing the traditional Australian damper, perfect because of its simplicity, with native Australian flavours. My 'Central Australian' themed dampers reflect the flavours of the desert regions around Alice Springs, and can be served with lemon myrtle oil, saltbush dukkah or sticky bush tomato balsamic glaze to create a unique confluence of flavours.

Athol Wark, Alice Springs, Northern Territory

MAKES 12 ROLLS

3 cups self-raising flour, sifted, plus extra for sprinkling
½ cup powdered milk
1 teaspoon roasted ground wattleseed or ground bush tomato (kutjera), plus extra for sprinkling (see note)
pinch of salt
½ cup butter, cubed, at room temperature
300 ml water

Preheat the oven to 180°C. Grease and flour a baking tray.

Combine the flour, powdered milk, wattleseed or bush tomato and salt in a large bowl. Using your fingertips, rub in the butter until combined. Gradually add the water, mixing until the ingredients are well combined and the mixture is smooth, and not dry.

Place the dough on a floured bench top and knead briefly. Divide the dough into 12 small rolls. Place on the baking tray, score the tops, sprinkle with extra flour and spice and cook for 20–25 minutes, or until golden brown.

Note: Ground wattleseed and bush tomato can be found in some specialty provedores or purchased online.

SUN MUSCAT GRAPE PICKLE

Sun Muscat is a variety of grape grown in the Sunraysia region of north-west Victoria, which produces 90 per cent of Australia's dried fruit. When the grapes are harvested in March and April, some of the fruit gets left on the vine. Rather than leave the fruit to rot, I decided to find a use for it and came up with this pickle recipe. I use the Sun Muscats rather than the sultana grape as they give the pickle a lovely muscatel flavour. This pickle is delicious with cold meats, or simply with cheese and dry biscuits. The jars will keep for about 12 months in the pantry — but these pickles are so yummy I doubt they will last that long!

Roslyn Hudson, Merbein, Victoria

MAKES 12–15 500 ML JARS

500 g cooking salt
5 litres water
2 kg onions, coarsely chopped
2 kg Sun Muscat grapes, picked from their stems
5 cups white vinegar
3 cups sugar
1 cup plain flour
3 tablespoons mustard powder
1 tablespoon ground turmeric
2 teaspoons curry powder
1 teaspoon cayenne pepper

Make a brine the day before cooking. Mix the salt and water in a clean plastic bucket and add the onion.

The next day, transfer the onion and half of the brine to a large stockpot and add the grapes. Bring to the boil and boil for 10 minutes. Discard the other half of the brine.

Drain the grapes and onion and rinse thoroughly under cold water to remove all the salt. Drain well.

Bring the vinegar and sugar to the boil in a large saucepan over high heat. Boil, stirring, until the sugar is dissolved. Remove from the heat.

Combine the flour, mustard powder, turmeric, curry powder and cayenne pepper in a medium bowl. Gradually add 1 cup water, stirring, to make a thin paste.

Add the curry paste to the vinegar mixture and stir to combine. Add the drained grapes and onion. Return the saucepan to a low heat and allow the mixture to simmer for 20 minutes.

Remove the saucepan from the heat and allow the pickle to cool a little. Bottle in labelled sterilised jars. Store in a cool, dry place and refrigerate once opened.

LEWIS PRINCE

Little Prince Eating House & Bar, Traralgon, Victoria

In the regional Victorian town of Traralgon, chef Lewis Prince says these days consumers increasingly want to know where their food comes from. 'We're more than happy to talk about where our meats, vegetables and eggs are sourced — we source local wherever possible,' he says. He adds that giving customers that knowledge is important as it helps to support small suppliers, creates jobs and increases food sustainability.

Every item on his menu adds a distinctive element — a sourness or sweetness; a crunch or softness — but ultimately the purpose of every dish is to promote thought and get people talking.

In his dish, Lewis has chosen to showcase Gippsland ingredients, particularly asparagus, which is grown extensively in the area. In peak season, around 70 per cent of asparagus found in supermarkets will have been grown in Gippsland.

The secret of the dish is in his sauce. Lewis has developed his own version of XO — a spicy seafood sauce that is a relatively new addition to China's ancient culinary repertoire. XO sauce has a history shrouded in mystery. It originated in Hong Kong and is commonly used in most southern Chinese regions. He says it's a great recipe for home cooks as once you've made it, it lasts a long time — 'It can stay in your fridge for one to two months if you preserve it by covering it with oil' — and you can serve it with a multitude of vegies or steamed fish. The list of combinations is endless.

The base sauce can be as hot or as mild as you like. 'The ingredients for the sauce are a combination of shallots, garlic, chilli, dried shrimp and scallops, and you can either use pork belly, or, as in this instance, jamón or prosciutto. Lewis fries the ingredients off in vegetable oil, and then cooks them down to caramelise and develop their flavours. Then all you need to do is blanch your asparagus and toss it in the XO sauce. Keep it quick, simple and fresh.

GIPPSLAND ASPARAGUS IN XO SAUCE

SERVES 6

MAKES ABOUT 500 G XO SAUCE

3 bunches asparagus, peeled to just before the tips, woody ends trimmed
50 g fried shallots, for garnish
5 spring onions, thinly sliced, for garnish

XO SAUCE
75 g dried shrimp
1 cup vegetable oil, or just enough to cover all the ingredients
150 g dried scallops, sliced
75 g garlic (about 20 cloves), finely chopped
75 g shallots (about 6), finely chopped
150 g jamón or prosciutto, finely shredded
25 g fresh long red chillies (about 6), deseeded and finely chopped
15 g dried long red chillies, soaked, deseeded and finely chopped
7 g dried bird's eye chillies, finely chopped
15 g sugar, or to taste
1 tablespoon fish sauce

To make the sauce, pour ½ cup hot water over the dried shrimp in a small bowl and set aside to soak for 2 hours.

Drain the shrimp, reserving the soaking water, and pat dry with paper towel. Set the shrimp and soaking water aside.

Heat half the oil in a wok or large saucepan over medium heat. Add the scallops to the wok or pan and fry, covered with a lid to protect yourself from the spitting oil, for 1–2 minutes or until crisp. Drain well on paper towel.

Pour the oil from the wok into a heatproof container and wipe out the wok with paper towel. Return the reserved oil to the wok, add the remaining oil and heat over medium heat. Add the garlic and shallots and cook, stirring continuously, for 4–5 minutes, or until golden brown.

Add the jamón or prosciutto, and fresh and dried chillies, and cook for a few seconds (be careful, it may burn easily). Add the rehydrated shrimp, fried scallops and reserved soaking water, and stir continuously for a few more seconds. Add the sugar. Cook for 20–30 minutes, stirring occasionally, until fragrant and the water is completely evaporated. Add the fish sauce and stir, and remove the sauce from the heat. Transfer to a large heatproof bowl.

Put the asparagus in a large saucepan of boiling water. Cook for 20 seconds and transfer immediately to a bowl of iced water. Drain and add the asparagus to the bowl with the XO sauce. Toss 4–5 times until all the asparagus is coated. Remove from the bowl and place on a large serving plate. Garnish with the fried shallots and spring onions and serve immediately.

Note: Dried shrimp can be found in Asian grocery stores. The leftover XO sauce will keep in an airtight container in the fridge for 1 month.

MALLEE SMASHED CHICKPEAS

Grown here under the big sky of the Mallee, this golden crunchy legume is very versatile. This recipe was created to inspire Australians to experiment with dried chickpeas and entice the local farmers who grow it to consume this flavoursome gem. Experience the wonderful flavour and texture of Mallee smashed chickpeas and consume to your heart's content on savoury biscuits or crusty bread, with vegetable sticks, in sandwiches or on your favourite hamburger with a dash of relish. If you don't have access to your very own supply of dried chickpeas, ask around or head to the local supermarket.

Marianne Ferguson, Hopetoun, Victoria

SERVES 6 AS A SIDE DISH

1 cup dried chickpeas
1 chicken or vegetable stock cube
juice of 1 lemon
2 garlic cloves, coarsely chopped
3 heaped tablespoons mayonnaise
drizzle of olive oil

Place the dried chickpeas in a slow cooker and cover with boiling water. Add the chicken or vegetable stock cube, cover and cook on high for 3½ hours until cooked but still firm to the bite (see note).

Drain the chickpeas, place in a large bowl and refrigerate until cool.

Add the lemon juice, garlic, mayonnaise, a good drizzle of olive oil and salt and pepper to taste. Use a stick blender and blend until the ingredients are combined and the chickpeas are 'smashed' — they should be rough and irregular rather than puréed.

Cover and store in an airtight container in the fridge. Serve as a dip or spread, as desired.

Note: If you don't have a slow cooker, put 1 cup dried chickpeas and 2 cups water in a saucepan and soak overnight. In the morning, add a stock cube and boil the chickpeas for 30 minutes (or up to 1 hour for a softer result).

BANANA SALAD

Easter holidays at Dunk Island almost 10 years ago, camping with four of my children, was a great adventure. One special experience was enjoying boom netting on the island ferry and indulging in a helping of banana salad afterwards. And, living in Cairns, what better to serve up at a meal than a no-cook side dish packed with healthy local ingredients? I use locally grown bananas and coconut, Mungalli natural Greek-style yoghurt and Australian almonds. The best thing about this dish is that if any is left over after the main course, you can add extra fruit and a scoop of ice cream and you have dessert covered. No family get-together is complete without our banana salad.

Chris Williams, Cairns, Queensland

SERVES 5–6

10 bananas, peeled and sliced
juice of 1 lemon
500 g natural Greek-style yoghurt
½ cup freshly shaved coconut
50 g slivered almonds, toasted

Place the banana in a large stainless steel bowl. Sprinkle the lemon juice over and gently mix through.

Spoon the yoghurt over and gently mix through to coat the banana. Sprinkle the coconut and almonds over the top and toss gently until combined.

Transfer to a serving bowl and serve.

BALLARAT SILVERBEET TART

The area may be famous for gold, but there's also some great local produce available around Ballarat, and an ever-increasing slow-food culture. This original tart recipe includes some of the best ingredients available in central Victoria. For the pastry I used Powlett Hill flour brought home by my husband after shearing sheep on the Campbelltown property. For the filling I purchased silverbeet from Spring Creek Organics in Navigators, free-range Green Eggs from Great Western and Creswick-grown garlic from the Lake Wendouree Smart Living Market. However, I think the Meredith Dairy marinated goat's cheese and Mount Zero kalamata olives from the Grampians are the heroes of the dish. Even my fussy children will eat it!

Jean Flynn, Ballarat, Victoria

SERVES 6

1½ cups plain flour
100 g cold butter, cubed
2–4 tablespoons cold water

FILLING
1 tablespoon olive oil
¾ bunch silverbeet (leaves and stalks), chopped
2 garlic cloves, finely chopped
½ cup grated parmesan cheese
16 kalamata olives, pitted and halved, plus extra, to serve
2 eggs, lightly beaten
150 g marinated goat's cheese
sliced or quartered tomatoes, to serve

To make the pastry, put the flour in a large bowl and rub the butter in using your fingertips. Gradually add the water and mix using a butter knife to form a dough. Bring together to make a disc and wrap in plastic wrap. Refrigerate for 30 minutes.

Meanwhile, make the filling. Heat the oil in a large frying pan over medium heat. Add the silverbeet stalks and cook, stirring, for 5 minutes, or until soft. Add the garlic and silverbeet leaves and cook, stirring occasionally, for a further 10–15 minutes, or until the leaves are wilted. Season with salt and pepper. Set aside to cool.

Preheat the oven to 180°C.

Lightly grease a 24 cm tart tin. Roll the dough out on a floured bench top to a circle large enough to fit the base and side of the tin, and carefully line the tin with the dough. Spread the parmesan evenly over the dough base and top with the cooked silverbeet and the olives. Pour the beaten egg over the filling and crumble the goat's cheese over the top.

Bake for 30–35 minutes, or until cooked through and golden on top. Serve warm with fresh tomatoes and extra olives.

EMMA LUPIN

Taste of the Top End website, Darwin, Northern Territory

Emma Lupin was very excited when she heard about this cookbook, as she's been committed to promoting the growth and use of local food in Darwin for several years. 'This concept is so important because 97 per cent of our fresh produce (and 100 per cent of dried) travels more than 3000 km to get to us.' Because of this, Emma has dedicated herself to educating residents about growing their own food.

Emma's food philosophy is that food is central to every culture and every community. She started her website, Taste of the Top End, to tell the story of the food that she produces on her block in Alawa, and to inspire others to follow suit. Emma went on to develop and co-manage a wonderful project called 'Growing and Understanding Local Produce (GULP) NT'. The project brings together culturally diverse members of the Darwin community to share their valuable knowledge of local foods through workshops and an online recipe/story resource.

Her food philosophy also revolves around living sustainably and being as kind to the local environment as possible, and she carries this ethos into her other pursuits — as a conservation worker, she coordinates Land for Wildlife, a voluntary program for locals who want to manage their block as a habitat for native animals.

For *Australia Cooks*, Emma has created a Roasted rainbow salad of green paw paw and Top End dry-season garden produce to showcase the paw paw, an ingredient that is abundant in the Darwin region and is incredibly versatile. 'Best of all,' she says, 'paw paw can be roasted when still green — it is an amazing vegie with a peppery flavour.'

Her recipe combines paw paw with other local vegetables such as eggplant, which grows abundantly all year, as well as zucchini and capsicum, which grow during the dry season. She says, 'The flavours come from local herbs including five-in-one herb and lemon basil, as well as local chillies and ginger — also easy to grow all year.' But, she adds, you can use any seasonal vegetable that is available to create this wonderfully fresh dish.

ROASTED RAINBOW SALAD OF GREEN PAW PAW AND TOP END DRY-SEASON GARDEN PRODUCE

SERVES 3–4

olive or coconut oil for stir-frying
1 cm piece ginger, peeled and finely chopped
1 small bunch spring onions or garlic chives, chopped
500 g green (but just about to turn) paw paw, cubed
2 long eggplants, cubed
1 fresh long red chilli, whole
1 capsicum, cubed, or 1–2 tomatoes, cubed
1 medium zucchini, cubed, or 3–4 yellow or green 'flying saucer' squash
1 small five-in-one herb leaf (also known as tropical oregano or Spanish sage)
1 small bunch lemon or purple basil, chopped

Preheat the oven to 180°C. Line a baking tray with baking paper.

Heat a little oil in a wok or large frying pan over medium–high heat. Add the ginger and spring onion or garlic chives, and cook until soft. Add the paw paw and cook for 3–4 minutes. Add the eggplant, chilli, capsicum or tomatoes and zucchini or squash, increase the heat to high and stir-fry for 2 minutes or until lightly browned. Toss through the five-in-one leaf and basil, reserving some basil for garnish, and season with salt and pepper to taste.

Transfer the paw paw and vegetables to the baking tray and cook in the oven for 20 minutes or until cooked through.

Serve warm in bowls garnished with the reserved basil.

VEGETARIAN SAVOURY LUPIN PANCAKES

The flour I use to make this recipe is made from 100 per cent Australian sweet lupins — the iconic pulse of Western Australia. In fact, 85 per cent of the world's sweet lupins are produced in this state. My Indian-inspired savoury pancakes are made by combining lupin flour with chickpea flour and vegetables, and adding a wonderful zing of ginger, chillies, turmeric and coriander leaves. Lupins are the world's richest source of combined protein and fibre, with negligible starch, and they are gluten-free. They add a new dimension to healthy eating — as do these exotic and delicious pancakes.

Dr Shyamala Vishnumohan, Coorow Seeds, Coorow, Western Australia

MAKES 10

½ cup lupin flour (see note)
½ cup chickpea flour
½ small onion, finely diced
¼ tomato, finely chopped
½ cup mixed vegetables (e.g. mashed potato, finely diced carrots, zucchini, capsicum)
1 teaspoon grated ginger
1 teaspoon red chilli powder
¼ teaspoon ground turmeric
¼ cup chopped coriander leaves, plus extra, to serve
canola oil spray
yoghurt, herbed sour cream and/or a tomato relish, to serve

Place all of the ingredients except the oil, yoghurt, sour cream and tomato relish in a large bowl and stir to combine well. Season with salt to taste and set aside for 15 minutes.

Add up to ¾ cup water a little at a time, mixing as you go, to make a batter slightly runnier than a pancake batter. As there is no gluten in this batter, you don't have to worry about making the pancakes tough through overmixing.

Heat a well-seasoned cast-iron or non-stick frying pan over medium heat and spray lightly with oil. Pour ¼ cup of the batter into the centre with a rounded ladle and spread slightly with the bottom of the ladle to get an even-looking circle. Cook on medium heat until the sides dry up and the bottom of the pancake turns golden brown. Flip over and cook until the other side turns golden brown. Keep the pancakes warm as you cook the remainder.

Serve hot with the extra coriander leaves and yoghurt, herbed sour cream and/or a tomato relish.

Note: Lupin flour can be found at some health food stores. If you can't find it, use 1 cup of chickpea flour instead of ½ cup.

ROASTED VEGETABLE AND FETA PIES

We cook these pies often for our B&B guests; vegetarians love them, as do most meat-eaters. Use whatever combination of seasonal, local produce you like — it will always result in beautiful flavours. I purchase most of the ingredients in the Gympie region — Fat Hen Farm olive oil, Kenilworth Cheese Factory feta and Cooloola cream, for starters. These pies are best eaten the day after they are made, as the flavours develop, and they are perfect cold for a picnic or lunch.

Tanya Fisher, Melawondi Spring Retreat, Imbil, Queensland

SERVES 6

2 cups coarsely chopped pumpkin
2 small zucchini, coarsely chopped
1 red onion, coarsely chopped
1 small capsicum, coarsely chopped
1 large or 2 small eggplants, coarsely chopped
2 garlic cloves, skin left on
3 tablespoons extra-virgin olive oil
5 free-range eggs
165 g good-quality feta cheese, crumbled
¾ cup full-fat cream
½ cup grated parmesan cheese
green salad, to serve

PASTRY
1⅔ cups plain flour
125 g chilled butter, chopped
1 egg
chilled water, if needed

Preheat the oven to 200°C. Line a baking tray with baking paper.

To make the pastry, process the flour, butter and egg in a food processor until it combines to form a ball, adding a little chilled water if necessary. Wrap the pastry ball in plastic wrap and refrigerate for 1 hour.

Meanwhile, combine all of the vegetables and the garlic in a large bowl. Splash the oil over, season with sea salt and black pepper and toss the vegetables to evenly coat them. Transfer to the baking tray. Cook in the oven for 35 minutes, or until cooked through. Remove the vegetables from the oven and set aside to cool. Pick out the garlic cloves and set aside.

Lightly grease six 10 cm springform tins. On a floured bench top, knead the pastry slightly and roll it out as thinly as possible. Line the tins with the pastry, pushing it into the bases and trimming the edges. Prick the bases a couple of times with a fork.

To blind bake, line the pastry with baking paper and weigh down with baking weights or uncooked rice. Bake in the oven for 15 minutes, remove the baking weights and return the pastry to the oven to bake for a further 10 minutes, or until lightly brown. Leave in the tins.

Put the eggs, feta, cream and parmesan in a large bowl. Squeeze in the roasted garlic and combine gently. Add the vegetables and stir to coat. Spoon the mixture evenly among the pastry shells.

Bake for 35–40 minutes, or until the centre of the pies are cooked through. Remove from the oven and allow to cool for 5 minutes, then release and let the pies cool completely on a wire rack. Serve warm or cold with a fresh green salad.

BAKED PUMPKINS

We have a pecan farm in the Dumaresq Valley, and our pecans are definitely the stars in this recipe. We use beautiful pumpkins from the farm next door, garlic from the Liverpool Plains, and baby spinach and rosemary from our garden. It is healthy, tasty, very cheap (especially when the pumpkins are free!) and looks spectacular.

Annabelle Hickson, Bonshaw, New South Wales

SERVES 2 AS A MAIN COURSE, OR 4–6 AS A SIDE DISH

2 small whole pumpkins
oil, to fry
2 garlic cloves, finely chopped
1 red onion or 1 leek (whatever is in the house), finely chopped
2 sprigs rosemary, leaves removed and finely chopped
100 g brown rice
75 g currants
100 g pecans, roughly chopped
300 ml good-quality chicken stock
generous handful of baby spinach
zest of 1 lemon
sour cream, to serve

Cut the tops off the pumpkins and set aside. Scoop out the seeds and discard. Scoop out a little of the pumpkin flesh to make each hollow slightly larger. Finely chop the scooped-out pumpkin.

Heat a dash of oil in a large frying pan with a lid over medium heat. Add the chopped pumpkin, garlic, onion or leek and rosemary and cook, stirring occasionally, for 10 minutes, or until the onion or leek and pumpkin are soft (rather than fried and brown). Add the rice, currants and pecans and cook for 3 minutes. Add the stock and cook, covered, for 35 minutes. Add the spinach leaves and allow to wilt.

Preheat the oven to 180°C.

Tear off 2 sheets of foil large enough to wrap the pumpkins and place on 2 baking trays. Place the pumpkins, cut side up, on the foil. Fill the pumpkin hollows with the rice mixture, including the cooking liquid from the pan. Replace the pumpkin tops.

Bring the foil up the side of the pumpkins to wrap them. Tear off 2 more sheets of foil, place them over the pumpkins and wrap them completely. Transfer the pumpkins on the baking trays to the oven. Cook for 1 hour, or until you can easily pierce the pumpkins with a knife (the cooking time will vary according to pumpkin size).

To serve, slice wedges of the whole pumpkin and scatter over the lemon zest. Serve with a dollop of sour cream.

KIRBY SHEARING

Soul Projects, Mount Gambier, South Australia

Chef Kirby Shearing has a different story to tell when it comes to supporting his local food producers and growers. Kirby is the director of catering and events company Soul Projects, and has developed a strong reputation off the back of his passion for fine dining.

Kirby's food philosophy is 'to create dining experiences with a modern edge, and use fresh, regionally sourced produce with a story that links land to table and ocean to plate'.
Kirby also conducts personalised tours for foraging food lovers; he's often found somewhere along the coast near Port MacDonnell, looking for succulent, salty bower spinach or vibrant green stalks of samphire, which is similar to crisp baby asparagus. He also keeps an eye out for useful ingredients such as coastal parsley and saltbush. Along the Limestone Coast, there are over 90 wild ingredients for Kirby to choose from. However, running a successful business has its challenges, and he doesn't always have the luxury of time to forage.

It's easy to say 'buy local', but it's not always possible to put this ethos into practice in such a remote location. Kirby says many local growers are encouraged to sell their produce to the city markets, making it even harder to source locally. He bases a good portion of his menus around the produce grown by his good friend Taryn Ward in her market garden one kilometre north of town, and also uses organic produce from other local towns such as Kalangadoo, Naracoorte and also Millicent.

Kirby's dish demonstrates his respect for fresh garden produce and local artisan products. He's combined roasted carrots and beetroot, fried carrots and parsnips, pureed peas with olive oil and a pumpkin cheese made with feta from the Limestone Coast Cheese Company to create 'From the garden'. 'I really love this dish as it is one that changes with the seasons on our menus. Really, it's a dish that reflects what can be foraged, farmed and found throughout the year within a 50 km radius from my kitchen. It has textural elements and also a raw earthy taste, beautiful colours and, with the addition of flowers, smells like a spring garden.'

FROM THE GARDEN

SERVES 10

oil for deep-frying
40 g leek, green part only
550 g yoghurt
3 sprigs mizuna, nasturtium and fennel fronds per plate
good-quality sourdough bread, sliced, to serve

PURÉED ROASTED CARROTS AND BEETROOT
500 g carrots
500 g beetroot
30 g unspun honey
240 ml olive oil
300 ml water
2 star anise
16 black peppercorns
6 sprigs thyme
1 cinnamon stick

DEEP-FRIED CARROT AND PARSNIP
2 large carrots
2 large parsnips

PURÉED PEAS
250 g fresh peas
50 ml olive oil

PUMPKIN CHEESE
1 small butternut pumpkin
475 g Persian feta

Preheat the oven to 200°C.

To roast the carrot and beetroot, place them in separate small baking dishes, distribute the honey, olive oil, water and spices evenly between both dishes, season with sea salt and seal tightly with foil. Cook the carrot in the oven for 25 minutes, and the beetroot for 90 minutes.

As the carrots and beetroot are cooked, respectively, remove from the oven and allow to cool slightly. (Keep the oven on to cook the pumpkin.) Peel by rubbing the skins off with your hand. Purée the cooked carrots and beetroot separately in a blender, adjusting the seasoning with salt only. Cover and chill in the fridge.

Heat the oil for deep-frying in a medium saucepan or deep-fryer to 165°C. For the fried carrot and parsnip, slice as thinly as possible using a mandoline or V-slicer. Cook separately in small batches in the preheated oil in the saucepan or deep-fryer until crisp (the oil will stop bubbling and the parsnip and carrot will colour rapidly). Drain on paper towel separately. Set aside 3 rounds of parsnip per plate and crush the remainder using a small blender. Reserve all the carrot.

For the puréed peas, bring a small saucepan of water to the boil. Add the peas and cook for 2 minutes, then drain and transfer immediately to a bowl of iced water to stop the cooking. Drain the peas and purée in the blender with the olive oil and a little water if necessary. Season the purée with salt and chill in the fridge for at least 2 hours.

Meanwhile, for the pumpkin cheese, cook the pumpkin whole in the oven for 1–1½ hours or until a knife can be easily inserted. Cool slightly, and peel and chop roughly, discarding the seeds. Purée the cooked pumpkin to a fine pulp in a blender. Strain the feta, chop roughly and blend with 200 g of the pumpkin purée until smooth. Cover the pumpkin cheese and remaining pumpkin purée in separate bowls and place in the fridge.

For the leek tops, cook until charred under a grill or in a hot oven. Blitz in a blender or spice grinder with enough salt to create a fine 'ash', about 2–3 teaspoons.

To plate, use piping bags to pipe randomly placed even amounts of all the purées, pumpkin cheese and the yoghurt on 10 serving plates. Scatter the parsnip crumb over some items, and dust others with the leek ash. Scatter the fried parsnip and carrot slices around each dish. Garnish the plate with the mizuna, nasturtium and fennel fronds, and serve with some sourdough bread.

BEGA VALLEY BRUNCH CHEESE TART

The Bega Valley on the New South Wales far south coast has been known for its dairy products for over a century. To give homage to these products — including Tilba milk, cream and parmesan, and Bega butter and tasty cheese — I have put together a recipe for a cheese tart that combines these products with the organic tomatoes and herbs grown in the Bega Valley region. Eat this great tart hot or cold for brunch. It also freezes well.

Wendy Goodisson, Stony Creek, New South Wales

SERVES 6

BASIC HOT MILK PASTRY
¼ cup full-cream milk
60 g butter, cubed
1 cup self-raising flour

TOMATO TOPPING
olive oil, to drizzle
500 g roma tomatoes, cut in half lengthways
2 handfuls of coarsely chopped herbs e.g. basil, oregano, marjoram (what you have in the garden is always best), plus ½ bunch basil, extra
25 g parmesan cheese, coarsely grated, plus extra, to sprinkle

CHEESE FILLING
150 ml thick clotted cream or 125 g mascarpone cheese
2 egg yolks, lightly whisked
50 g parmesan cheese, grated
250 g shredded tasty cheese

To make the pastry, microwave the milk and butter in a heatproof plastic bowl on high for 1 minute, or until the butter has melted. Add the flour and mix until the dough forms a ball. Knead the dough on a floured bench top. Wrap the dough in plastic wrap and refrigerate for 30 minutes.

Preheat the oven to 160°C. Lightly grease a 24 cm tart tin. Roll out the pastry between two sheets of baking paper until it is large enough to fit the size of your tin. Line the pastry with baking paper and weigh down with baking weights or uncooked rice, and blind bake in the oven for 15 minutes. Remove the baking weights and return to the oven to bake for a further 10 minutes, or until golden. Set aside.

Increase the oven temperature to 180°C. Line a baking tray with baking paper.

Place the tomatoes on the baking tray. Drizzle with oil and scatter over the chopped herbs. Top with the parmesan, and season with sea salt and a few grinds of black pepper. Cook in the oven for 10 minutes, or until brown on top. Set aside to cool, and reduce the oven to 170°C.

To make the cheese filling, combine the cream or mascarpone cheese, egg yolk, parmesan and tasty cheese in a medium bowl.

Line the pastry shell with a layer of fresh basil leaves. Spoon the cheese mixture on top and arrange the tomato halves on top of the cheese mixture. Sprinkle with a little extra grated parmesan and cook for 35 minutes, or until the cheese mixture is firm when tested with a skewer.

Allow to cool slightly before cutting.

UPSIDE-DOWN RATATOUILLE

The Riverland region of South Australia is blessed with an abundance of beautiful fresh fruits and vegetables all year round that can be purchased directly from producers' roadside stalls or local farmers' markets. The region also produces great wines, premium olive oil and fine balsamic vinegar. We call this savoury variation of the tarte tatin 'upside-down ratatouille' for obvious reasons. Enjoy it with a simple salad and a light Riverland red or crisp chilled Riverland rosé on a summer's night …

Debra & Christophe Tourenq, Berri, South Australia

SERVES 4–6

3 tablespoons olive oil
3 large brown onions, sliced
2 garlic cloves, sliced
½ small red chilli, halved
2 teaspoons fresh thyme leaves, plus 1 extra teaspoon, to sprinkle
4 roma or other small–medium tomatoes, cut in half lengthways
1 large zucchini, cut in 1 cm slices
1 medium eggplant, cut in 1 cm slices
balsamic vinegar, to drizzle
Murray River pink salt
freshly ground black pepper
2 tablespoons chopped fresh basil, plus extra, to garnish
½ tablespoon chopped fresh rosemary
1½ sheets puff pastry
1 egg yolk, beaten

Heat 2 tablespoons of the oil in a saucepan and cook the onion, garlic, chilli and thyme on low–medium heat for 20–30 minutes, or until the onions are soft and caramelised. Remove from the heat and set aside.

Meanwhile, preheat oven to 180°C.

Place the tomato, zucchini and eggplant on a baking tray, drizzle with balsamic vinegar and the remaining olive oil, and season with the salt and pepper. Roast for 20 minutes or until golden brown. Remove the vegetables from the oven and increase the temperature to 200°C.

Grease a shallow baking dish or tray and line with baking paper. Place the tomatoes, cut side down, in the dish with the zucchini and eggplant so they all fit nicely side by side. Scatter the caramelised onion and fresh herbs over the top.

Place the pastry over the vegetables and trim if necessary, leaving enough to tuck in around the inside edges of the dish to completely cover the vegetables. Brush the pastry with the egg yolk.

Bake for 20–25 minutes or until the pastry is a nice golden brown colour.

Place a board or serving dish large enough to cover the baking dish and flip it upside down. Remove the baking paper, sprinkle with the extra thyme and basil leaves, *et voilà!*

PUMPKIN & ASH CHÈVRE TORTELLINI WITH CITRUS BEURRE NOISETTE

This recipe brings back fond memories of making pasta with my Polish grandma, parents and brother. The combination of the tart goat's cheese, sweet pumpkin, delicate beurre noisette sauce and orange is a match made in heaven. I like to use a beautiful Faudel Farmhouse ash chèvre goat's cheese, which I came across at the Warragul Farmers' Market.

Kylie Szeremeta, Gippsland, Victoria

SERVES 3–4 (MAKES 16 TORTELLINI)

100 g plain flour, plus extra, to dust
1 egg
50 g butter
1 cup diced pumpkin
1 garlic clove, crushed
1 tablespoon orange marmalade
50 g ash chèvre goat's cheese
3 sprigs thyme, finely chopped, plus extra sprigs, to garnish
2 teaspoons dukkah or finely chopped nuts and seeds
squeeze of lemon juice
baby pansies and thyme tips, to garnish (optional)

Place the flour, egg and a pinch of salt in an electric mixer with a dough hook and mix on high until a dough is formed and comes away from the side, adding a small amount of water if necessary. Don't mix for too long as your pasta will become tough.

Place the dough on a floured bench top and bring together into a ball with your hands. Coat well with flour and wrap in plastic wrap. Place in the fridge for 30 minutes or longer.

Heat a teaspoon of the butter in a frying pan over medium heat. Add the pumpkin and garlic and cook gently until the pumpkin starts to turn pale. Add half the marmalade and cook for 10–15 minutes, or until the pumpkin begins to caramelise. Transfer the pumpkin mixture to a food processor and pulse until you have a chunky purée. Add the goat's cheese and thyme, and season with salt and pepper. Pulse again until just combined. Transfer the mixture to a bowl, cover and pop in the fridge.

Remove the dough from the fridge, gently flatten it and cut it in half. Using a pasta machine on the largest setting, roll out one half of the dough. Coat the dough generously with plain flour on both sides and continue to roll through the pasta machine, reducing the thickness each time, down to about a 3–4 thickness.

Place the pasta strip onto a floured surface and cut out 7.5 cm circles with a pastry cutter. Take the pumpkin filling out of the fridge and place a small amount in the centre of each circle. Dab a small amount of water around the edge of the pasta and fold in half, gently sealing the edges and ensuring no air is left inside. Carefully wrap the semicircle around your pinky finger and seal the pointy edges together. Don't worry if your tortellini don't look perfect — you will get better with practice. Place the tortellini on a floured plate, and continue until you run out of dough and/or filling.

Bring a large pot of salted water to the boil. Cook the tortellini in batches for 3 minutes, or until they float to the top. Transfer to a colander when cooked and drizzle with a little oil to prevent them from sticking together.

Melt the remaining butter in a medium frying pan over medium–high heat. Add the extra thyme sprigs and dukkah and continue to cook until the butter starts to turn golden brown and begins to smell nutty. Quickly add the lemon juice and remaining marmalade and remove the pan from the heat. Add the pasta to the butter sauce and toss until well coated. You can garnish the dish with edible flowers and thyme tips if you like.

SOPHIE ZALOKAR

Foragers, Pemberton, Western Australia

A cook with a passion for local food is out to show that a small town at the bottom end of Western Australia has surprises for those who look. Truffles, potatoes, apples, brassicas, fish from nearby Windy Harbour, even saffron — Sophie can quickly tick off a list of her local foods without having to think. The menu at her Pemberton restaurant, Foragers, is table d'hôte and the seating is communal. Locals mix with visitors and the stage is set for revelations.

When asked about the concept of foraging, Sophie says it's much more complex than it is in Europe. You have to be respectful of the regulations and Indigenous cultural connections to foraging in the bush. The exception to the rule is introduced weeds. 'We pick watercress at the Lefroy Brook and purslane [a succulent weed used in fattoush] in a friend's garden.'

Top chefs stress the importance of local and seasonal ingredients, and Sophie is no exception. The rural community of Pemberton loves to share; 'wonderful boxes of this and that' are regularly left on the doorstep, and will often find their way onto that night's menu. The local culinary heritage also plays a part in the way that Sophie develops a recipe. Buckwheat is a good example: 'In this area, we have a few northern Italian families. They brought buckwheat with them. It's a weed that survives in the harshest of conditions.' As such, buckwheat has become a signature product of the area; Sophie sources it from two kilometres down the road to create meals with a regional flair.

Despite being tucked away near the south coast, the 50-seat restaurant is often fully booked, with a waitlist. 'Word of mouth is powerful,' says Sophie. She and her husband have had the property for 10 years now. Sophie doesn't play down the success of the business, which includes accommodation and cooking classes. She says hospitality is not an easy industry. However, in her estimation, Pemberton is the most well-kept secret in WA's tourism catalogue. 'People, place and produce are the important ingredients, mixed with the authentic experience so sought after by travellers.'

Sophie's love of cooking with local signature ingredients is showcased in this beautiful Beetroot, buckwheat and boursan tarte tatin, made with delectable Cambray cheese produced in Nannup, less than 100 kilometres away.

BEETROOT, BUCKWHEAT AND BOURSAN TARTE TATIN

SERVES 8

1 tablespoon olive oil
25 g butter
500 g golfball-sized baby beetroot, tops removed, scrubbed
1 tablespoon apple cider vinegar
1 tablespoon soft brown sugar
1 cup pre-cooked buckwheat kernels, also called kasha (optional, see note)
120 g Cambray Boursan cheese, or a fresh-style goat's cheese
2 handfuls radicchio leaves, washed and torn into bite-sized pieces
2 tablespoons best-quality aged balsamic vinegar
2 tablespoons toasted pine nuts, for garnish
¼ cup flat-leaf parsley leaves, for garnish

PASTRY
180 g wholemeal self-raising flour
70 g buckwheat flour (see note)
200 g unsalted butter, diced
½ teaspoon salt
½ cup Greek-style yoghurt

To make the pastry, place the flours, butter and salt in a food processor and pulse until the mixture resembles coarse breadcrumbs. Add the yoghurt and continue to pulse until the dough just begins to combine. Turn out onto a lightly floured bench top and gently compress the dough together into a flattened ball. Wrap in plastic wrap and refrigerate for 15 minutes.

Preheat the oven to 180°C.

Heat the oil and butter over medium heat in an ovenproof frying pan large enough for all the beetroot to fit snugly in a single layer. Add the beetroot and toss to coat in the oil and butter. Evenly sprinkle over the vinegar, sugar and a little sea salt and freshly ground black pepper. Cover the pan with foil and cook in the oven for 40–50 minutes or until the beetroot are just tender when pierced with a skewer. Allow to cool for 20 minutes.

Roll out the pastry until 5 mm thick and cut out a circle a little larger than the pan. Spoon the pre-cooked buckwheat kernels over the beetroot to fill the gaps, if using. Carefully place the pastry over the top and tuck the excess pastry into the inside edge of the pan. Return the pan to the oven and cook for 25–30 minutes or until golden. Remove from the oven and set aside to rest for 5 minutes.

To serve, place a large plate over the pan and carefully, but quickly, turn upside down. Evenly place dollops of the Cambray Boursan cheese on top and surround the edge of the tarte tatin with the radicchio leaves. Drizzle over the balsamic and garnish with the pine nuts and parsley leaves. Grind over some freshly ground black pepper and serve.

Note: Pre-cooked buckwheat kernels and buckwheat flour can be found in some health food stores.

From the Sea

From the creeks, rivers and lakes to the seas that surround us, Australian waters provide us with an array of stunning seafood: oysters, marron, mud crabs, prawns, and an amazing variety of fish, to name only a few. It's just one more reason why we're the lucky country.

Nothing tastes quite like fresh seafood. When I was talking to Matthew Evans about his book *The Gourmet Farmer Goes Fishing*, he tried to describe the taste of just-caught squid to me. Sweet, soft, salty freshness that melts in the mouth ... He eventually gave up. We decided that, unless you have been lucky enough to taste it, it's impossible to describe, but once you've experienced it you will never forget it.

Famed chef Tony Bilson once told me how grateful he was to learn from an Indigenous tribe how to cook a mullet over a fire and then run it quickly through fresh seawater to bring out the taste of the sea. You don't have to do much to good seafood — just respect it.

Use these recipes as inspiration. When choosing your seafood, talk to your local fishermen and seafood purveyors and ask about origin and fishing techniques or aquaculture methods, so that you can make informed, sustainable seafood choices.

And have fun discovering the endless array of local ingredients that you can combine with your seafood to make it shine.

GRILLED TASSIE OYSTERS WITH SMOKED SALMON AND CAMEMBERT

This 15-year-old recipe is a delicious way to eat our wonderful oysters. I came up with it when a friend wanted oysters and couldn't handle them Kilpatrick, and now I will never eat them any other way. I use only Tasmanian oysters, of course, as well as Huon Valley smoked salmon and King Island camembert.

Dee Hasell, Huonville, Tasmania

SERVES 3–4

500 g rock salt
12 oysters, freshly shucked
1 punnet cherry tomatoes
4 teaspoons mayonnaise
4 teaspoons French dressing
100 g smoked salmon, cut into 12 pieces
200 g camembert cheese, cut into 12 pieces
¼ green capsicum, thinly sliced
¼ red capsicum, thinly sliced
1 avocado, sliced, to serve

Preheat the grill to medium–high heat. Cover a baking tray with foil and scatter over the rock salt. Place the oysters and cherry tomatoes on the tray and use a few cherry tomatoes to help balance the oysters so they are not leaning to one side — this will help the cheese cook evenly under the grill.

Dab or drop a little mayonnaise and dressing, about ⅓ teaspoon of each, onto each oyster. Top with a piece of smoked salmon to cover the oysters, and then a piece of camembert, and thin slices of green and red capsicum.

Cook the oysters under the preheated grill until the cheese bubbles and is golden.

Serve as an entrée with the grilled tomatoes and slices of avocado on the side.

REDCLAW CRAYFISH AND AVOCADO SALAD WITH DILL DRESSING

We have been farming the redclaw in ponds here at Proa Station, south-east of Julia Creek, since 1999. Redclaw is a species of freshwater crayfish that is native to all rivers in the Gulf of Carpentaria, and found to be suitable for aquaculture ventures. We use artesian water in our ponds, which we have been told adds to the flavour of our redclaw. We are proud of our product; the tail meat is very versatile, and has a sweet, delicate and unique flavour. Redclaw is even sometimes referred to as 'champagne lobster'. When we cook redclaws en masse, we first stun them by submerging them in iced water. We then cook the redclaws in boiling salted water for about 8 minutes, and then immediately plunge them into a salted ice slurry. This last step is the most important as it cools the redclaws quickly, stopping the cooking process. Other seasonal fruits such as mango can be added to the salad to give it another dimension. Enjoy!

Judy Fysh, Julia Creek, Queensland

SERVES 4–6

1 mignonette lettuce, leaves separated
2 kg cooked redclaw crayfish, peeled
2 ripe avocados, sliced
1 small nectarine, thinly sliced

DILL DRESSING
300 g sour cream or Greek-style yoghurt (for a healthier option)
1 cup mayonnaise
1 cup French dressing
2 tablespoons chopped chives
2 tablespoons chopped dill

Spread the lettuce over a serving plate and arrange the redclaw, avocado and nectarine on top.

Whisk together all the dressing ingredients and drizzle over the salad.

Note: You can store any leftover dressing in an airtight container in the fridge for up to 1 week.

BEER-BATTERED POPCORN MARRON WITH LEMON CHILLI MAYONNAISE

Several years ago I made this recipe using marron caught from our own dam for a friend's birthday. The pleasant bitterness of the beer batter (and I like to use a good-quality bitter) goes well with the light tang of the mayonnaise, while the marron flavour is captured within the crisp bready coating. To add to the local nature of this dish, the lemon came from the tree in our orchard, the chilli is from our herb garden, the eggs were laid by our free-range chickens and the honey is from nearby Nannup.

Murray Rose-Jones, Wilgarrup, Western Australia

SERVES 4

2 cups self-raising flour
¾ cup bitter beer
2 egg yolks
1 cup olive oil
zest and juice of 1 lemon
1 teaspoon honey
1 kg marron
oil for deep-frying
sesame seeds, to sprinkle
1–2 red chillies, seeded and finely sliced, to sprinkle (optional)
mayonnaise, to serve

To make the batter, place 1 cup of the flour and a pinch of salt in a medium bowl. Add the beer, stirring, until it has the thickness of a cake mixture. Set aside.

To make the mayonnaise, place the egg yolks in a medium bowl. Beating with electric beaters, slowly add the oil until well incorporated. Stir in the zest and lemon juice, to taste (for a light tang rather than too sour), and the honey. Add a pinch of salt, if desired. Refrigerate until needed.

Pre-cook the marron for 4–6 minutes in boiling, unsalted water (as a guide, 4 minutes for a 250 g marron and 6 minutes for a 500 g one), or until the head and body shells have separated. Drain and set aside to cool. Remove the flesh from the shell and the claws, and cut into 1 cm square pieces.

Heat the oil for deep-frying in a large saucepan over high heat. (Place a clean wooden spoon handle in the oil and when it starts to bubble, the oil is ready for cooking.)

Place the remaining flour in a bowl and dust the marron lightly, shaking off any excess flour. Dredge the marron in the batter and then drop into the oil, a few pieces at a time (don't crowd the pan). Remove when golden brown and puffed to double their size. Place on paper towel to drain.

Place the marron pieces in a large serving bowl, sprinkle with sesame seeds and chilli, if using, and serve with a bowl of mayonnaise for dipping.

CRAIG SQUIRE

Ochre Restaurant, Cairns, Queensland

When some of the country's finest produce can be grown or caught on your doorstep, there is no need to look any further afield. Such is the philosophy of Far North Queensland chef Craig Squire: 'With the wet tropics on the coast and the high Tablelands with its cool climate, we have the greatest variety of foods grown in Australia, and it's all within about a 100 km radius of Cairns.'

As the executive chef and director of Ochre Restaurant in Cairns, Craig has spent years perfecting recipes that highlight the abundance of ingredients available in the region, particularly those which are native to Australia.

His love of native foods began in his home town of Adelaide, before he made the move to the Sunshine State. 'There was a lot more gourmet food development [in Adelaide] 25 years ago; I found that coming to Far North Queensland was like stepping back in time in terms of the cultural development of cuisine.'

Seeing the potential of the region's food industry, Craig formed industry groups to inspire and encourage producers and restaurateurs to move with the times. In the 21 years he has lived and worked in the Far North, he has watched with pleasure as the region's food industry has matured into what it is today. 'The food industry has certainly come a long way here and it's been a pleasure to be able to support local products and to help it grow,' he says. He's particularly proud that the region is now able to produce its own chocolate, made from cocoa, dairy and sugar all grown within a small radius.

In his recipe, Craig uses a raft of native ingredients including Gulf of Carpentaria bugs, lemon myrtle and macadamia nuts. His favourite hot and sweet chilli paste is Australian Rainforest Plum and Berry Jeowbong made by local provedore Rainforest Bounty, but says other soy chilli pastes will also work well. 'It's actually quite a simple recipe, but it really encapsulates the flavours of Far North Queensland.'

TEMPURA BUGS WITH GREEN PAPAYA SALAD AND LEMON MYRTLE AND SWEET CHILLI DIPPING SAUCE

SERVES 4 AS AN ENTRÉE

8 fresh lemongrass stalks
8 pieces green bug meat
lemon myrtle and sweet chilli dipping sauce, to serve (see notes)

TEMPURA BATTER
150 g packet tempura batter mix (see notes)
oil for deep-frying

GREEN PAPAYA SALAD
1 small green papaya, peeled, seeded and cut into long matchsticks
50 g green beans, cut into 2.5 cm pieces
40 g unsalted roasted macadamias
½ red onion, thinly sliced
12 cherry tomatoes, cut in half
10 g fresh mint, chopped
10 g fresh coriander, chopped

NAM JIM DRESSING
2 small green chillies, thinly sliced
2 garlic cloves, thinly sliced
¼ cup lime juice
60 g palm sugar, grated
¼ cup fish sauce
30 g hot and sweet chilli paste, such as Australian Rainforest Plum and Berry Jeowbong
1 teaspoon sea salt

Cut the lemongrass stalks on an angle at the point where the stem starts to branch. Skewer a piece of bug meat onto each stick of lemongrass. Set aside.

Combine all the ingredients for the green papaya salad. Combine all the ingredients for the nam jim dressing and toss through the salad.

Prepare the batter according to the packet instructions.

Heat the oil to 180°C in a large saucepan or deep-fryer.

Dip the bug skewers in the batter and deep-fry for 4–6 minutes, or until golden and cooked through. Drain on paper towel.

Place the papaya salad on four serving plates, place the bug skewers next to the salad and serve with the dipping sauce on the side.

Notes: You can find lemon myrtle and sweet chilli sauce at some specialty provedores, or make your own by adding ground lemon myrtle leaf to sweet chilli sauce, to taste.

Tempura batter mix can be found in Asian grocery stores.

BARBECUED OYSTERS WITH GRILLED POTATOES AND SAMPHIRE

All ingredients for this dish are from the SAGE Farmers Market in Moruya, where all produce must come from within a 160 km radius. The oysters are from the Oyster Coast — an oyster trail running 300 km along the pristine coastline of the New South Wales south coast, and the world's most sustainable oyster industry. The samphire and the warrigal greens are foraged. Both are native plants that grow along the eastern and southern coasts of Australia. The samphire adds a salty, citrus flavour as well as a crunch. It's an easy dish to assemble at the last minute around the barbecue, but the oysters need to be watched closely to make sure they don't overcook — get them off the heat as soon as they open.

Stuart Whitelaw, Bingie, New South Wales

SERVES 4–6

¼ cup hazelnuts
500 g waxy potatoes, scrubbed and cut into 1 cm slices
3 garlic cloves, chopped
4 tablespoons extra-virgin olive oil
300 g zucchini, halved lengthways and thinly sliced
½ bunch spring onions, sliced diagonally
½ cup samphire
100 g warrigal greens, tips only, blanched and refreshed in cold water
24 unshucked oysters
juice of 2 limes, plus extra wedges, for garnish

Notes: Samphire and warrigal greens can be found at some specialty provedores and farmers' markets.

If you can't find samphire, you could use small green beans, blanched and refreshed, or raw kohlrabi matchsticks. Add extra lime juice and salt to compensate for the samphire.

If you can't find warrigal greens, you could use spinach.

Preheat the oven to 170°C. Place the hazelnuts on a baking tray lined with baking paper. Cook for 10 minutes. Remove and rub off the skins with a tea towel. Chop coarsely and set aside.

Parboil the potato slices for 4 minutes, or just until the potato starts to soften.

Combine the chopped garlic and olive oil in a small bowl. Heat 1 tablespoon of the oil and garlic in a medium frying pan over medium–high heat and stir-fry the zucchini, spring onion and half of the samphire for 3–4 minutes, or until the zucchini begins to colour. Add the warrigal greens and stir to warm through. Season with sea salt and the lime juice, and set aside.

Preheat the barbecue grill. Brush the parboiled potato slices with the remaining oil and garlic mixture and place on the grill.

Place the oysters on the grill until they just open, then remove from the heat immediately.

To serve, arrange the grilled potato on a serving plate and spoon the stir-fry mixture into the middle. Scoop out the just-cooked oysters from their shells along with their liquid and spoon on top of the vegetables. Garnish with the reserved samphire and lime wedges and the chopped hazelnuts.

FLATHEAD CEVICHE WITH ACHACHA AND BLACK QUINOA SALAD

The achacha is a tropical fruit that originates in the Amazon Basin of Bolivia. I co-manage Palm Creek Plantation, which is located 45 km south of Townsville and is the largest commercial achacha orchard outside of Bolivia — in fact, we believe we have more fruiting trees than there are in Bolivia! The plantation is chemical-free and uses natural processing farming methods. Achacha has been described as 'sweet, tangy, refreshing and sorbet-like'. It is somewhat similar to mangosteens, longans, rambutans and lychees; however, it has only one-third the sugar of these other fruits. It can be frozen for use in the off-season, either in its skin or by freezing the pulp. Achacha blossom honey is highly sought after by honey aficionados. The combination of achacha, pomegranate and quinoa make this ceviche of lime-cured fish with a tropical dressing even more fascinating. You'll need 8–10 limes all up. Colourful and refreshing, this dish is a true reflection of our Burdekin region, which is brimming with vibrant produce and seafood.

Helen Hill, Giru, Queensland

SERVES 2 AS A MAIN COURSE OR 4 AS AN ENTRÉE

1 tablespoon salt
300 g flathead fillet or other sustainable reef fish, skin removed and cut into 2 cm cubes
¾ cup lime juice
500 g fresh achacha
1 cup cooked black quinoa
mint leaves, to serve
¼ red onion, finely chopped, to serve

SALAD
1 avocado, finely chopped
½ red capsicum, finely chopped
1 small cucumber, cut in half lengthways, seeds removed with a spoon and finely chopped
¼ cup steamed corn kernels
seeds from ½ pomegranate
1 red chilli, finely sliced (optional)

DRESSING
2 tablespoons achacha blossom honey or similar
1 tablespoon apple cider vinegar
¼ cup lime juice
chilli sauce, to taste

Mix the salt with ¼ cup water and rub the solution into the flesh of the fish. Drain the fish and transfer to a glass bowl. Add the lime juice and the pulp from 10 achachas (remove the seeds by squeezing between your fingers and thumb) to the bowl and toss the fish to coat well. Cover and allow to marinate in the fridge for 10–15 minutes. Cover with just-boiled water to remove the acid, and leave to steep for 20 minutes. Pat dry.

Meanwhile, make the salad. Place the avocado, capsicum, cucumber, corn kernels, pomegranate seeds and chilli, if using, in a large bowl. Toss gently to combine.

Place the dressing ingredients in a jar with a lid and shake to combine. Pour three-quarters of the dressing over the salad and toss well.

Pile the black quinoa in the centre of each plate, and scatter a little around the edge. Place the salad on top of the quinoa. Scatter the marinated fish cubes over the salad. Drizzle over the remainder of the dressing, and scatter over the mint leaves and the onion. Serve immediately.

Tip: Slice the achacha skins and place in a jug with water and ice for a refreshing drink to serve with your meal.

HUW JONES

Zanzibar Café, Merimbula, New South Wales

Chef Huw Jones and Renee Loftus have owned and operated Zanzibar Café for 4 years, and have invested much of that time forming relationships with local fishermen, farmers and gardeners. 'It's our aim to serve our diners as much produce from the surrounding areas as we can,' says Huw. Local ingredients on the Zanzibar menu include organic lamb and beef from Bombala, free-range pork, free-range eggs and pasture-raised rabbits. There is also an abundance of local seafood, including oysters, mussels, abalone, freshwater eels, sea urchin, and of course a wide variety of fish. 'I chose to use sea urchin for my recipe as it is a somewhat unknown and underutilised ingredient that grows in abundance, and is environmentally friendly and sustainable.'

Local divers Keith Brown and Andrew Curtis are the men behind South Coast Sea Urchins, the company which supplies Zanzibar's sea urchins. They've set up a sustainable fishing program which includes selective hand harvesting, meaning they take only those urchins that are viable for processing and leave the rest. Sea urchins are known for their ability to strip rocks bare by devouring weeds and algae in fisheries. Keith and Andrew have found that harvesting them commercially has rehabilitated the ocean floor. 'When we thin out [the sea urchins], the abalone move in, and when they move in, they spawn and establish new colonies of abalone. And the amount of fish has increased. It's quite noticeable,' says Keith. 'If we continue the program, we'll see quite a substantial change in biodiversity.'

Keith says that while there is a strong Asian market for sea urchins, they can be an acquired taste. 'When I taste with people from Melbourne, they say it's like a scallop and when I taste with people from Sydney, they say it's like an oyster. So if you're halfway between those, you're pretty right.'

Eating a raw sea urchin has been described as sharing an intimate kiss with the ocean, and Huw has penned his love letter to the sea urchin in his recipe for Buckwheat pikelets with Sapphire Coast sea urchin roe, creamed eggs and bottarga. Huw suggests serving this dish as a canapé, or in larger portions as part of brunch.

BUCKWHEAT PIKELETS WITH SAPPHIRE COAST SEA URCHIN ROE, CREAMED EGGS AND BOTTARGA

SERVES 4

100 g crème fraîche or sour cream
200 g sea urchin roe (see notes)
2 tablespoons finely sliced parsley or chives
2 tablespoons grated bottarga (see notes)

CREAMED EGGS
4 free-range eggs
2 tablespoons mayonnaise (preferably home-made)
1 tablespoon crème fraîche or sour cream
sea salt and white pepper, to taste

BUCKWHEAT PIKELETS
½ cup buckwheat flour (see notes)
½ cup self-raising flour
pinch of salt
¾ cup milk
1 free-range egg
butter, for frying

To make the creamed eggs, place the eggs in a saucepan of cold water over high heat and bring to the boil. Turn the heat as low as it will go and cook the eggs for a further 7 minutes. Drain the eggs and place them straight into a bowl of iced water to chill.

When the eggs are cool, peel them and pass them through a fine sieve, or mash them well with the back of a fork in a small bowl. Add the mayonnaise and crème fraîche or sour cream, mix to combine and season to taste with salt and white pepper. Cover and place in the fridge until ready to serve.

To make the buckwheat pikelets, sift the two flours and salt together into a large bowl. Whisk together the milk and egg in a small bowl. Make a well in the flour and slowly add the milk mixture, stirring until you have a smooth and lump-free batter. Set aside for 15 minutes.

Heat 1 teaspoon of butter in a medium frying pan over medium heat until foaming. Add tablespoonfuls of the batter in rounds and cook until bubbles form on the surface. Flip and cook the other side for another 20 seconds. Transfer the pikelets to a plate lined with paper towel as you cook them.

To serve, spoon a teaspoon of the creamed egg mixture onto each pikelet and top with a small dollop of crème fraîche or sour cream and sea urchin roe. Scatter with the parsley or chives and bottarga.

Notes: Sea urchin roe can be found in some specialty seafood provedores.

Bottarga, which is salted and cured fish roe, can be found in some specialty seafood provedores, but if you can't find it, salmon or trout roe can be used in its place.

Buckwheat flour can be found at some supermarkets and health food stores.

MAROOCHY RIVER MUD CRAB CAKES

We live on the beautiful Maroochy River and regularly catch nice muddies at our doorstep. Our herb garden is home to a good Ceylon spinach plant that grows prolifically to provide plenty of greens. You can serve it with these crab cakes, which are easy and quick to prepare. This dish works well as an entrée or main meal — depending on how many you can eat! It's a family favourite in our house.

Andy Leach, Maroochydore, Queensland

SERVES 4 AS AN ENTRÉE

250 g mud crab meat
⅔ cup spring onions, finely chopped
½ cup finely chopped coriander leaves, stems and roots
3 tablespoons dried breadcrumbs
3 tablespoons cornflour
1 egg, lightly beaten
2 tablespoons fish sauce
good pinch of salt
½ teaspoon freshly ground black pepper
coconut oil, for shallow-frying
Ceylon (or English) spinach leaves, to serve
sweet banana chilli, seeded and thinly sliced, to serve
lime cheeks, to serve

DIPPING SAUCE
3 tablespoons sweet chilli sauce
1 tablespoon lime juice
2 teaspoons fish sauce

Place the crab meat, spring onion, coriander, breadcrumbs, cornflour, egg, fish sauce, salt and pepper in a large bowl. Mix thoroughly.

Form the crab mixture into 12 small flat patties with your hands and place on a baking tray lined with baking paper. Cover with plastic wrap and place in the freezer for 30 minutes, or until firm.

Meanwhile, make the sauce by combining the chilli sauce, lime juice and fish sauce in a small bowl.

Heat ½ cm coconut oil in a medium frying pan over medium heat. Shallow-fry the crab cakes in batches for 1–2 minutes on each side, or until golden. Remove from pan, place on paper towel to drain and keep warm.

Place the spinach leaves on small plates and top with 3–4 crab cakes per person. Sprinkle over the sweet banana chilli slices and serve with the lime cheeks and the sauce on the side.

HONEY FISH

In the Gulf of Carpentaria we are in a unique position to enjoy delicious fresh seafood from both the Gulf Rivers and the ocean. And enjoy it we do, in so many ways. This dish, for example, originated when we had guests staying at our resort for a week from Leeton, New South Wales. On their last night, with no other guests, they told us to relax and they would cook dinner. They served us Honey fish, and we have been cooking it ever since! It combines our local seafood with a regional Asian influence, and it's an absolute taste sensation, plus it showcases how new friends can cement a friendship with food. It's also a great way to get kids or fussy non-fish eaters to try and enjoy fish. Make sure to keep the temperature of your deep-frying oil high to ensure a crisp batter. Another tip is to mix a big jar of soy and honey and leave it in the fridge to thicken slightly, as the thicker consistency will help it coat the battered fish better. And why the big jar? Because once you've tasted this, you will want to make it again!

Lyn Battle, Sweers Island, Queensland

SERVES 8–10

2 cups self-raising flour
1 teaspoon bicarbonate of soda
pinch of salt
1 kg white firm-fleshed fish fillet (whatever is in season), cut into 1.5 cm cubes
oil for deep-frying
½ cup honey
¼ cup soy sauce
sliced spring onions, for garnish
sesame seeds, for garnish
shaved fresh coconut, for garnish (optional)

Combine the flour, bicarbonate of soda and salt in a large bowl. Add 2 cups cold water and whisk well. Add the fish to the batter and toss to coat well.

Heat the oil in a large saucepan over high heat and allow to get nice and hot. (Place a clean wooden spoon handle in the oil and when it starts to bubble, the oil is ready for cooking.) Using tongs, put the fish pieces into the hot oil, a few pieces at a time, moving them around for about 1–2 minutes, or until cooked and golden on both sides. Drain on paper towel and transfer the fish to a large bowl.

Combine the honey and soy sauce by putting them in a jar and giving it a good shake.

Spoon the mixture over the fish and gently toss it to coat evenly. (Mixing with a flat spoon protects the fish from breaking.)

Transfer the fish to a serving plate and garnish with the spring onion, sesame seeds and coconut, if using.

FORAGED SHELLFISH IN CREAMY CIDER SAUCE

Nothing sums up the rugged Victorian south-west like fresh seafood and the creamiest dairy. This region produces the very best of both, I think, and this recipe combines the two in a feast fit for any chilly southern night. Celebrating foraged seafood, this dish includes world-renowned black-lipped abalone and goes some way to combating the invasive spread of the (delicious) wakame seaweed. Both are available for free and in abundance — all that's needed is the fortitude to brave the cold waters of the coast. Make the butter and cream the local Warrnambool brand, and use Bellarine Peninsula apple cider. Best served fresh over an open fire on the beach!

Chris Lewis, Torquay, Victoria

SERVES 4

250–300 g pippis
1 legal-sized black-lipped abalone (see note)
800 g–1 kg fresh mussels
50–100 g wakame seaweed
60 g butter, plus extra, to serve
4 shallots or 1 small brown onion, coarsely chopped
1 long red chilli, finely chopped
2 garlic cloves, finely chopped
2 thyme sprigs
150 ml thickened cream
250 ml apple cider
fresh crusty bread, to serve

To prepare the pippis, place in a small covered container of salted water and leave for 1 hour. The pippis will spit out any gritty sand, leaving beautifully sweet flesh.

Shuck and clean the abalone, and remove the gonads. Slice the cleaned flesh finely into thin strips.

Debeard and scrub the mussels.

Rinse the wakame under cool water. Finely slice it into long strips.

Melt the butter in a large frying pan or wok with a lid over medium heat. Add the shallots, chilli, garlic and thyme and cook, stirring. Once the shallots turn translucent, reduce the heat to low and add the cream and cider, stirring to create a sauce. Leave to simmer for 2–3 minutes.

Increase the heat to medium and add the mussels, stirring thoroughly to coat with the sauce. Cover with the lid and leave to steam for 2 minutes — the mussels should be starting to open and have a brilliant orange colour.

Add the abalone, pippis and wakame, and stir so they are completely covered in the sauce. Cover and cook for another 2 minutes, or until all the pippis are open and bright white.

Remove the pan from the heat and spoon the seafood into bowls with generous amounts of the sweet and creamy sauce. Serve with fresh crusty bread, extra butter and a cold bottle of cider (or two).

Note: Fresh and frozen abalone can be found in some specialty seafood provedores.

TERRY FIDLER

Brisbane Street Bistro, Launceston, Tasmania

With over 40 years in hospitality, chef Terry Fidler of Brisbane Street Bistro says Tasmania has some of the best locally grown produce in the country, with a wealth of meat, fish, poultry and dairy that is world-class — though it is perhaps lacking in tropical fruits. He says, 'I love our seafood, particularly wild-caught seafood off Tasmania. We don't have a massive variety, but what we have is very good.'

While Brisbane Street is French in style, Terry thinks the approach to Tasmanian produce needs to be simple and holistic. 'The vegetables are perfect, the meat is perfect — don't be too fussy,' Terry advises. 'I don't like things that have got too many different flavours; I like to keep it simple.'

Before working in Launceston, Terry owned and operated several different restaurants on Tasmania's east coast and he admits it is a challenging area for the hospitality industry. 'You don't see the restaurants in Tasmania that you see in other parts of the world, because we don't have the population.' Terry says nearly 70 per cent of chefs wash out before they're 30. 'You have to be prepared to give up a lot if you want to be any good. It's a choice you have to make.'

With reality TV cooking programs topping the ratings across the country, Terry thinks attitudes to food have changed in recent years, and for the better. 'I hope it continues, perhaps not at the breakneck speed it's been in the last few years … The more people are aware of what they're eating and where it's from, the better it's going to be.'

In his recipe, locally caught octopus is cooked sous vide to make it beautifully tender. If you don't have a vacuum sealer, he advises cooking the octopus without the bag in a well-covered baking dish in the oven at 75°C for 3–4 hours. The octopus is then paired with a wasabi mayonnaise, saffron potatoes, almond crunch, charred red capsicum and a salsa verde to create a wonderfully complex and textural salad.

CONFIT OF OCTOPUS SALAD WITH SAFFRON POTATOES, ALMOND CRUNCH AND SALSA VERDE

SERVES 6–8

1 large (about 1 kg) octopus, cleaned, legs separated, head discarded
200 ml olive oil
200 ml chardonnay vinegar
1 teaspoon sea salt
1 teaspoon sugar
1 teaspoon freshly ground black pepper
1 red capsicum
watercress, for garnish

WASABI MAYONNAISE
1 teaspoon wasabi
1 teaspoon rice wine vinegar
2 egg yolks
pinch of sea salt and freshly ground black pepper
150 ml grapeseed oil

SAFFRON POTATOES
400 g Dutch cream or Bintje potatoes, peeled and cut into 2 cm dice
pinch of saffron threads
20 g sugar
20 g salt
200 ml olive oil

ALMOND CRUNCH
100 g butter
100 g almonds, coarsely chopped
100 g stale bread, finely diced

SALSA VERDE
6 anchovies, finely chopped
handful basil leaves, finely chopped
handful flat-leaf parsley leaves, finely chopped
2 tablespoons capers, rinsed, drained and finely chopped
4 roasted garlic cloves, mashed
30 ml chardonnay vinegar
50 ml olive oil

To cook the octopus using the sous-vide method, place the octopus in a vacuum food packaging bag with the oil, vinegar, salt, sugar and pepper. Extract the air, seal the bag and cook the octopus for 4 hours at 82°C. Cool the octopus in the bag in an ice bath.

To make the wasabi mayonnaise, place the wasabi, rice wine vinegar, egg yolks, and salt and pepper in a medium bowl. Whisk until well combined. Very slowly add the oil in a continual stream, continuing to whisk until the mixture is thick and creamy.

To make the saffron potatoes, combine the potatoes, saffron, sugar, salt, oil and 100 ml water in a heavy-based saucepan and cook, covered, over very low heat for 10–15 minutes or until cooked through, checking every few minutes that the potatoes aren't sticking. Drain all the liquid and allow the potato to cool.

To make the almond crunch, melt the butter in a medium heavy-based frying pan over medium heat. Add the almonds and bread, stir to combine and cook until the bread is crisp and golden. Transfer to paper towel to drain. Pulse the almonds and bread in a blender until you have a fine crumble. Set aside.

Char the capsicum with a blowtorch or over a gas burner until black. Place in a bowl, cover with plastic wrap and set aside to cool. Peel or scrape off the charred skin, remove the seeds and dice the flesh. Set aside.

To make the salsa verde, combine the anchovies, basil, parsley, capers and garlic in a medium bowl. Add the vinegar and oil, mix to combine and season with sea salt and freshly ground black pepper to taste.

To assemble the dish, remove the octopus from the bag, clean off the skin and suckers and cut into 2.5 cm pieces. Spoon the wasabi mayonnaise onto a serving plate and arrange the saffron potatoes, almond crunch, charred capsicum and octopus pieces on top. To serve, garnish with a little watercress and drizzle over some salsa verde.

CRISPY CORAL TROUT WITH BASIL AND CORIANDER PESTO

As a passionate third-year apprentice chef at the Townsville RSL, I love to study and create. For me, cooking is not only my career but my hobby as well. And being from the tropics, I love cooking coral trout because it is an iconic fish of the Great Barrier Reef and, being the main target species for reef line fishers along the Queensland coastline, it's the most popular fish in North Queensland. As for the herbs, I like to use basil and coriander for this recipe — basil is my absolute favourite. In tropical North Queensland we only have two seasons — hot and hotter — and whereas all other Mediterranean herbs seem to struggle with our humidity and wet seasons, basil is one-of-a-kind. Serve this dish with your favourite seasonal vegetables or, my personal favourite, a simple rocket salad with toasted cashews and pine nuts, drizzled with a basic vinaigrette.

Niccole Winfield, Townsville, Queensland

SERVES 4

olive oil, to cook
4 x 170 g coral trout fillets
micro herbs, to garnish

BASIL AND CORIANDER PESTO
1 cup basil leaves
¼ cup coriander leaves
1 garlic clove, chopped
2–3 tablespoons olive oil
1 tablespoon lemon juice

Heat a drizzle of oil in a non-stick frying pan over high heat. Season the fish with sea salt and freshly ground black pepper and place, serving side down, in the pan. Cook for 3–5 minutes, depending on the thickness of the fillets. Turn the fish and repeat on the other side. Turn the fish back over and reduce the heat to medium–low. Cook for a further 5 minutes.

Meanwhile, make the pesto by placing the basil, coriander and garlic in a blender. Season with salt and pepper. Pulse until coarsely chopped and, still pulsing, slowly add the olive oil and lemon juice. Add water, a teaspoon at a time, pulsing, until you are happy with the consistency.

Put the coral trout on 4 serving plates with the basil and coriander pesto drizzled over the top and garnish with your choice of micro herbs.

WATTLESEED AND BUSH PEPPER MURRAY COD WITH TOMATO AND CORIANDER SAUCES

The iconic Murray cod, quintessentially linked to the New England North-west region, was first described from specimens from Tamworth's Peel River (hence its scientific name *Maccullochella peelii*). It is still plentiful across the region, including in the beautiful Macdonald River downstream of Bendemeer. And with it in this recipe are the bush tucker specialties ground wattleseed and bush pepper, which together impart a beautiful smoky bush character to the fish, along with the tangy flavours of the Guyra tomato and coriander. Accompany the dish with a cool-climate, crisp white wine or boutique pale ale for which the New England region is becoming increasingly famous.

Joan Simms, Beechworth, Victoria

SERVES 4

2 teaspoons ground wattleseed (see note)
4 teaspoons ground bush pepper (see note), or ground black peppercorns
1 teaspoon ground sea salt
1 tablespoon extra-virgin olive oil
4 x 300 g Murray cod fillets or other white-fleshed freshwater fish, such as golden perch (yellowbelly) or redfin perch

TOMATO SAUCE
1 tablespoon extra-virgin olive oil
6 vine-ripened tomatoes, coarsely chopped
½ cup chopped onion
1 small red chilli, seeded and chopped
½ teaspoon lime juice

CORIANDER SAUCE
2 large handfuls fresh coriander leaves
2 tablespoons extra-virgin olive oil
ground sea salt and bush pepper, to taste

Combine the wattleseed, bush pepper and sea salt in a small bowl and use to coat both sides of the fish fillets. Set aside.

To make the tomato sauce, heat the oil in a large saucepan over medium–high heat. Add the tomato, onion, chilli and lime juice and bring to the boil, stirring to combine. Reduce the heat to low and simmer for 20 minutes, breaking down the tomato with a wooden spoon until the mixture is reduced and has become a smooth and thick sauce. Set aside.

To make the coriander sauce, place the coriander leaves and 1 tablespoon of the oil in a food processor or blender and blend until smooth. Heat the remaining oil in a medium frying pan over medium heat. Transfer the blended coriander to the pan and season with sea salt and bush pepper to taste. Cook for 5 minutes, stirring. Set aside.

Heat the oil in a medium frying pan over medium–high heat. Add the fish and cook for 2–3 minutes on each side, or until just cooked. Serve immediately with spoonfuls of the tomato and coriander sauces on each plate.

Note: Ground wattleseed and bush pepper can be found in some specialty providores, or purchased online.

SEAFOOD OMELETTE

How's this for great food made with fabulous local Bundaberg ingredients: Burnett Heads Ocean Pacific's spanner crab, Bundaberg Prawn Farm's black tiger prawns and XO Prawn Sauce, Grunske's local baby bug tail, Fig Tree Farm's open-range eggs, Bundy limes, and Walden finger limes from Mon Repos, where the turtles come in to lay their eggs. A sprinkle of gomashio, which is a combination of ground toasted black sesame seeds and sea salt, completes the flavour profile beautifully.

Amanda Hinds, Bundaberg, Queensland

SERVES 1–2

3 extra-large eggs
40 g butter
75 g green spanner or sand crab meat
75 g peeled green tiger prawns, deveined and halved lengthways
75 g shelled green baby bug tails, halved
15 g shiro (white) miso paste mixed with 100 ml hot water (see notes)
1 teaspoon XO sauce
juice of ½ lime
chopped spring onion, to serve
pinch of gomashio, to serve (see notes)
pulp of ½ finger lime, to serve (optional, see notes)
fresh Asian-style herbs, to serve (I use coriander and bush basil)
crusty white Vietnamese or French-style bread, to serve

To make the omelette, crack the eggs into a bowl and add 1 tablespoon water. Season with salt and pepper and whisk with a fork until combined.

Heat a medium frying pan over medium–high heat and add 10 g of butter. When the butter is sizzling, pour in half of the egg mixture and swirl to spread it over the base of the pan. When just cooked, roll the omelette over to form a cylinder and transfer to a serving dish. Cover with foil to keep warm. Repeat with remaining egg mixture.

Return the pan to the heat. Add the crab, prawns and bug tails and cook, tossing, for 30 seconds. Add the remaining butter, miso mixture, XO sauce and lime juice and cook for 2 minutes, tossing, or until the seafood is just cooked (it will keep cooking when removed from the heat).

Spoon the seafood and sauce over the rolled omelette. Scatter over the spring onion, gomashio, finger lime pulp, if using, and fresh herbs. Serve with fresh bread to mop up the juices.

Notes: Miso paste and gomashio can be found in Asian grocery stores.

Finger limes can be found at some specialty provedores and fruit markets between January and August. Finger lime trees can also be purchased online.

NOELLE QUINN

Qfood café, Albury, New South Wales

Chef and café owner Noelle Quinn has been a player and observer of her local food industry for some time. She grew up on a cattle and lamb farm in western Victoria and has spent 35 years in the industry in Albury Wodonga. She was also the coordinator of the Hume Murray Food Bowl, the organisation that introduced regular farmers' markets to the region. Over the years, she has noticed the varying influences on the food culture in the region.

'We had a strong European influence with the nearby Bonegilla Migrant Centre,' she says. The Bonegilla Migrant Centre was opened to help 'populate' Australia, and operated about 10 km outside of Albury Wodonga from 1947 to 1971. Over 320,000 migrants went through the centre, including those from Austria, Germany, Greece, Hungary, Italy, Yugoslavia and Spain.

But lately Noelle has been seeing a change. 'The increased number of migrants from Asian countries to the Albury Wodonga region in recent years is having an important and valuable influence on the local food industry,' she says. 'Over the years we have had an influx of Indian restaurants and Thai restaurants and now we are seeing some diversification on that; we have a Nepalese restaurant and there is a lot more Vietnamese influence in our community.' Noelle thinks the growing Asian presence has not only led to more choice for diners, but it is also starting to influence what local farmers are growing. 'One local farmer has added lemongrass, horseradish, ginger and garlic to his crops after asking people at farmers' markets and specialty food stores what shoppers were looking for,' she says.

At Qfood, Noelle serves a Vietnamese banh mi (meat and salad baguette), Vietnamese pho (soup), and pork and green papaya salad. 'What I serve comes from my own passion for and knowledge and understanding of Asian food, but the more we have served it and the clients have enjoyed it, the more it has become a stronger thread to what we do.'

Noelle's dish is Thai-inspired and uses seasonally available herbs, fruits and vegetables from her backyard garden and local farmers' markets.

CRISPY FISH FILLETS WITH TAMARIND SAUCE

SERVES 8

1–2 tablespoons peanut oil
8 x 240 g snapper or blue-eye fillets, skin on
banana leaf, to serve (optional)
3 red chillies, finely sliced
2 cups coriander leaves, picked and washed, to garnish
3 spring onions, julienned and refreshed in iced water, to garnish
steamed jasmine rice, to serve

TAMARIND SAUCE
6 tablespoons fish sauce
6 tablespoons lime juice
6 tablespoons tamarind paste
6 tablespoons palm sugar
6 tablespoons fried shallots
6 tablespoons fried garlic

To make the tamarind sauce, combine the fish sauce, lime juice and tamarind paste in a small saucepan over medium–high heat and bring to the boil. Add the palm sugar and a third of the fried shallots and garlic. Reduce the heat to low and cook, stirring, until the sugar has dissolved and the sauce thickens slightly. Set aside.

To cook the fish, preheat the flat plate on your barbecue or heat a good non-stick frying pan over medium–high heat. Add a very small amount of peanut oil, just enough to moisten the grill or pan, and place the fish firmly, skin-side down, onto the hot surface. Cook for 10 minutes or until there is no resistance when you press the thickest part of the fillets. If using a barbecue flat plate, use a metal scraper to slide it firmly under the crispy skin to ensure you remove it intact with the soft flesh.

Place the banana leaf (if using) on a serving plate and drizzle a little of the sauce on top. Position the fillets, flesh side down, on top of the sauce. Pour a little more sauce over the fish, and garnish with the chilli, coriander, spring onion and the remaining fried shallots and garlic.

Serve with steamed jasmine rice.

CREAMY FENNEL-INFUSED PRAWN, SCALLOP AND SALMON 'SEABREEZE'

Gippsland is produce and ingredient heaven for a home cook who runs cooking classes like me. I love where I live and it's difficult to choose a single food that signifies the region. My favourite local ingredients include Gippsland honey, Thorpdale potatoes, the magnificent seafood caught all the way from Lakes Entrance along the Ninety Mile Beach through to the Gippsland lakes, and the farmhouse cheeses from Maffra Cheese. Where I live in the Latrobe Valley I can access the open sea or the high country within an hour from my home. Surrounded by the bounty of rich soils, there are vegetables, fruit, beef, lamb, pork and poultry being nourished and prepared for our table, but on this occasion I have chosen to share what I call my 'Seabreeze' recipe that highlights the variety of fresh seafood available from Gippsland waters, which can be purchased from the seafood co-operative on the foreshore of Lakes Entrance.

Noelene Marchwicki, Churchill, Victoria

SERVES 4

6 tablespoons rice bran oil
2 red onions, sliced into thin wedges
6 fat garlic cloves, thinly sliced
3 salmon fillets (about 600 g)
1 small fennel bulb, thinly sliced (reserve the fennel fronds for garnish)
16 large prawns, shelled and deveined, tails left intact
250 g scallops
½ cup crème fraîche
50 ml ouzo (optional)
1 small red chilli, sliced
1 teaspoon freshly ground black pepper
steamed red rice, to serve (see note)

Heat 1 tablespoon oil in a large frying pan over medium heat. Add the onion and garlic and cook until softened and aromatic. Transfer to a bowl and set aside.

Add another tablespoon of oil to the same pan. Add the salmon and cook for 4 minutes each side, or until cooked through. Transfer the salmon to a chopping board and shred with two forks. Set aside.

Add a further tablespoon of oil to the same pan. Add the fennel and prawns, and cook for 2–3 minutes. Add the scallops and cook for a further 2–3 minutes, or until they are cooked through and turn white (this is a quick process). Transfer to the bowl with the onion and garlic and set aside.

Add the crème fraîche with the ouzo, if using, chilli and black pepper to the pan and reduce the heat to low. Add the shredded salmon and scallop and prawn mixture, stirring gently and allowing to heat through.

Transfer to a serving dish and garnish with fennel fronds. Serve with steamed red rice on the side.

Note: Red rice can be found at some supermarkets and health food stores.

GOLD COAST SURF 'N' SURF

Recently, I went out fishing with some mates and we managed to catch an 18 kg mahi-mahi, also known as dolphinfish. Mahi-mahi is pretty special — it has a firm white flesh with a delicate flavour, and it's so easy to prepare. The following day, I decided to give the mahi-mahi some special treatment. So, some shopping was in order — first to the trawlers, also known as the Gold Coast Fishermen's Co-op, for some beautiful fresh king prawns and cuttlefish, which I find has a much better flavour and texture than squid (and if you clean them then and there, there's no mess at home!). Next stop was the Racecourse Farmers' Market at Bundall for some fantastic organic produce from our hinterland: acid-free pineapples, mangoes, Mt Tamborine avocadoes, limes and herbs. Finally, I picked up a bottle of Vince Verdelho, made from grapes handpicked at O'Reilly's Canungra Valley vineyard. The result? An absolutely cracking meal!

Eric Carruthers, Gold Coast, Queensland

SERVES 4

4 garlic cloves, finely chopped
½ cup cold-pressed coconut oil
6 drops sesame oil
3 trawler-caught cuttlefish, cleaned
12 trawler-caught medium green prawns, 4 shelled and deveined, the rest left whole
4 x 200 g line-caught mahi-mahi steaks, skin on
½ cup plain flour, seasoned with salt, pepper and 1 teaspoon sweet paprika
coriander leaves, to serve
lime cheeks, to serve

PINEAPPLE MANGO SALSA
½ pineapple, peeled, cored and finely diced
1 mango, finely diced
1 red onion, finely diced
1 avocado, finely diced
½ red capsicum, finely diced
juice of 1½ limes
½ bunch coriander, leaves roughly chopped

Combine the garlic, ¼ cup coconut oil and the sesame oil in a medium bowl to make a marinade.

Prepare the cuttlefish by cutting open the tubes and scoring the flesh with a blunt knife. Add the cuttlefish (tubes and tentacles) and the prawns to the marinade and toss to coat. Cover and place in the fridge.

Meanwhile, to make the salsa, combine all of the salsa ingredients in a bowl and set aside.

Toss the mahi-mahi steaks in the seasoned flour to coat well, shaking off any excess. Heat the remaining coconut oil in a medium frying pan over medium heat. Add the mahi-mahi, skin side down, and cook for 3 minutes. Turn and cook until just cooked through. Transfer to a plate, season with salt and pepper and allow to rest (remembering the fish will continue to cook while resting).

Add the prawns to the frying pan, cook for 2 minutes and turn over. Add the cuttlefish, cooking until it turns white. Remove from the pan and season with salt and pepper.

Pile the pineapple mango salsa onto each plate, scatter with coriander leaves and place the seafood on top. Serve with lime cheeks on the side.

PETER KENT

Salt and Pepper Catering/Banrock Station, Riverland, South Australia

---

Sharing in his extended family's large Italian dinners brought home to chef Peter Kent the realisation that food is a way to bring people together. On Sunday evenings he would head to his sister-in-law's parents' place, where her mum and grandma had been cooking all day. 'I think that's where my real love of food came from — [seeing] their love for and knowledge of food.'

Peter moved to the Riverland with his wife, Lyn, 15 years ago and his cooking style was greatly inspired by the region's climate and produce. 'The climate is just so Mediterranean, and the food that is produced and grown here is beautiful in that sort of style.' Aside from running his own catering company, Peter is also executive chef at Banrock Station Wine and Wetland Centre. He prides himself on championing local produce, and creates just about everything on his menu from scratch; his philosophy is to keep it simple and let the flavours do the talking.

Peter credits Food Riverland with the improved promotion and range of the regional produce in recent years. Keen to increase the Riverland's food profile even more, he believes that the region needs to attract more tourists and in effect bring the rest of the world to the area, rather than exporting local produce outside of the region. 'I do a lot of dinners and cruises for international guests. When they get on the river and we serve them fresh local produce, they are blown away.'

Peter has designed this beautiful dish to represent the Riverland. The earthiness of the beetroot and horseradish combined with Murray River cod reminds him of the red sand meeting with the river; the saltiness of the cure along with the capers is the salt in the river; and the fresh citrus and gel is the sweet smell of orange blossom in the air. Peter is quick to add that the hard work of his local producers helps create this picture on the plate. The beetroot is from the Riverland Farmers' Market, the cod is from Parker's Cod Farm, the fresh orange juice is from Fat Goose Fruits, the bush limes and lemon myrtle are from Santalum Grove and he also uses Kolophon capers, Ollo olive oil and of course Murray River pink salt. 'I know the producers that we purchase from, and they have a love for their product that gets me excited about utilising it in original recipes.'

CURED MURRAY RIVER COD

SERVES 6

2 beetroot (about 200 g), trimmed and coarsely grated
375 g caster sugar
250 g rock salt
½ bunch dill, coarsely chopped
2 x 500 g sides skinless cod
2 oranges, segmented (juice reserved), to garnish
salmon roe, to serve
desert limes or limes cut into wedges, to serve
micro herbs, to serve

ORANGE GEL
250 g fresh orange juice
5 g agar agar

LEMON MYRTLE BRIOCHE CRUMBS
½ brioche loaf
1 teaspoon ground lemon myrtle leaf

CRISP CAPERS
oil for deep-frying
30 g salted capers, rinsed and drained

HORSERADISH CREAM
1 tablespoon grated fresh horseradish
1 cup crème fraîche

ORANGE VINAIGRETTE
¼ cup orange juice (reserved from the segmented oranges)
½ cup olive oil
½ teaspoon pink salt
pinch of freshly ground black pepper

Combine the beetroot, sugar, salt and dill in a large bowl. Place 2 sheets of plastic wrap, overlapping and long enough to enclose the cod, on a bench top. Spread half the salt mixture over the plastic wrap. Place the cod on top and pack the remaining salt mixture on top and around the fish. Wrap tightly in plastic wrap and place a tray on top to weigh it down. Refrigerate for at least 12 hours, turning halfway through. Wash the salt mixture off the cod thoroughly and pat dry. Slice very thinly and set aside.

To prepare the orange gel, bring the orange juice to the boil in a small saucepan and whisk in the agar agar. Allow to simmer for 1 minute, then remove from the heat and pass through a fine sieve into a bowl. Use a stick blender to blend until smooth and transfer the gel to a disposable piping bag. Set aside in the fridge.

To make the lemon myrtle brioche crumbs, tear the brioche into pieces and place in a food processor. Add the ground lemon myrtle leaf and process gently to obtain rough breadcrumbs. Spread over a baking tray lined with baking paper and lightly toast in the oven for 3–4 minutes. Set aside.

To make the crisp capers, heat enough oil for deep-frying in a deep-fryer to 160°C. Place the capers in a basket and fry for 1–2 minutes or until crisp. Drain thoroughly on paper towel and store in an airtight container.

To make the horseradish cream, combine the horseradish, crème fraîche and sea salt and freshly ground black pepper to taste in a bowl. Transfer to a disposable piping bag and set aside.

To make the orange vinaigrette, combine the orange juice, olive oil, salt and pepper in a small bowl. Taste and adjust the seasoning if necessary.

To serve, place the cured cod slices in the middle of a serving plate and top with orange segments. Dot the orange gel and horseradish cream around the plate. Sprinkle the crisp capers, salmon roe and desert limes or lime wedges around the plate, drizzle with the orange vinaigrette and finish with some lemon myrtle brioche crumbs and micro herbs.

From the Land

Nowadays, it's no longer just about steak and sausages — it's about delicious, lean kangaroo, tender lamb, succulent pork and so much more. With more people embracing a paddock-to-plate approach, the quality of meats is better than ever. Find out more about what's available in your backyard, and make the most of it with these incredible recipes.

On one episode of 'The Main Ingredient', chef Peter Gilmore, of Quay fame, reminisced about growing up in the 1970s watching his mum experimenting in the kitchen with many different cuisines — Italian, French, Chinese — and this multicultural culinary heritage, Peter said, has informed the way he now thinks about his food.

In this chapter, it's clear that home cooks have a similar understanding and respect for the diverse cuisines and ingredients now available to us. Some of these dishes — such as the Slow-cooked lamb shanks, or Roast pork shoulder with hazelnut and fig stuffing — are time-honoured, while others — like the Kangaroo dumplings and Berkshire pork on sugar cane skewers — are served up with a modern twist, showing we are open-minded and not weighed down by tradition or afraid of big flavours. The incredible diversity of dishes reflect a national style of cooking that is unique, yet honest.

You can prepare most of these recipes without having to be extremely skilled in the kitchen. I would encourage you to take a farm-to-table approach to your food. Talk to your local growers and producers, and cook with ingredients that are the very best your region has to offer. Once you choose good-quality local ingredients, they will do most of the work for you, making it a breeze to create beautiful food to eat with family and friends.

NICK AND SONIA ANTHONY

Masons of Bendigo, Victoria

Husband and wife chef team Nick and Sonia Anthony are all about cultivating relationships with local farmers and primary producers to create a direct link from the Central Victorian paddock to a very stylish plate, which is what makes their menu at Masons of Bendigo a unique expression of its location, environment and people. 'Central Victoria has developed in leaps and bounds over the last five years. The new generation of farmers are adopting new farming methods with the focus on quality rather than quantity; [their products] are the stars of our menu,' says Nick. The couple are surrounded by what they call 'food gold' from areas such as Inglewood, Tooborac, Heathcote, Boort and Harcourt, to name a few, and their menu is a showcase of delicious local goodies including olives and olive oils, heritage produce, artisanal cheese, beautiful vegetables and fruit, delicate micro herbs, and lovingly, sustainably produced meat.

Nick's Warialda Beef carpaccio with black pepper, beetroot, smoked aioli, kipfler chips and fried onion is a dish that combines his 20 years' cooking experience with Allen and Lizette Snaiths' 30 years' farming experience over at Warialda Beef. The Snaiths are passionate about nose-to-tail consumption, and this dish highlights the versatility of lesser-known cuts, which can be showstoppers if due care and respect is taken. Nick also uses extra-virgin olive oil from Saluté Oliva, eggs from 400 Acres, salt flakes from Pyramid Salt and herbs from B&B Basil, Victoria's largest micro-greens grower, also based in Bendigo. This dish is not as complex as it first may seem, and all the elements can be prepared ahead of time, with plating only taking a few minutes. Nick promises it's a dish that will wow even the most discerning dinner guest!

Sonia has also graciously passed on her recipe for baked lemon tart (page 264), a treasured recipe that she has been baking for family Christmas gatherings for the last decade. It's become so popular with the locals that she now also bakes it to help fundraise for the Bendigo Community Farmers' Market — in 2014 she managed to raise close to $2000. She says, 'It's an absolute hit — and how could it not be when you combine crumbly buttery pastry with velvety lemon custard made with local organic eggs, organic lemons and milk?'

WARIALDA BEEF CARPACCIO WITH BLACK PEPPER, BEETROOT, SMOKED AIOLI, KIPFLER CHIPS AND FRIED ONION

SERVES 4

250 g beef girello (see note)
2 tablespoons dijon mustard
4 tablespoons coarsely ground black peppercorns
3 tablespoons canola oil

SMOKED AIOLI
10 garlic cloves, peeled and smoked over wood chips
1 cup extra-virgin olive oil
2 teaspoons dijon mustard
3 egg yolks
30 ml white wine vinegar
salt flakes, to taste

FRIED SHALLOTS
1 cup canola or rice bran oil, for deep-frying
5 large shallots, peeled and thinly sliced into rings (a mandoline comes in handy here!)
½ teaspoon salt
½ teaspoon sugar

KIPFLER CHIPS
2 large kipfler potatoes, peeled and thinly sliced into rounds (a mandoline is good for this too)
vegetable oil reserved from frying shallots

GARNISHES
2 small target beetroots, washed and thinly sliced
Greek basil tops, frisée and young watercress, for garnish
sumac, to sprinkle
extra-virgin olive oil, to drizzle

Note: Beef girello, also known as 'butcher's eye fillet', is a cut traditionally used for corned beef. As the Warialda girello is of premium quality, there is a degree of fat marbling throughout the piece resulting in a product that is both tender and flavourful.

To prepare the beef, spread the mustard over the girello using a pastry brush. Place the ground peppercorns on a plate and roll the beef in them to coat both sides.

Heat the oil in a non-stick frying pan over high heat until smoking hot. Sear the beef very quickly on all sides and set aside to cool. Wrap tightly in plastic wrap, using about 11 layers, to create a cylinder shape. Set aside in the fridge.

To cook the garlic for the aioli, heat the olive oil in a medium saucepan to 80°C. Add the garlic and simmer until the cloves are soft, but without allowing to colour. Set aside to cool. Blend until smooth.

Blend the mustard, egg yolks and vinegar in a food processor. Slowly add the garlic oil, blending until the mixture emulsifies. If the mayonnaise is looking thick, add a dash of hot water before adding the remaining oil. Season to taste with salt flakes. Set aside in the fridge.

To make the fried shallots, heat the canola or rice bran oil to 120°C in a medium saucepan. Deep-fry the shallots until golden brown. Transfer to a large baking tray lined with paper towel. While still warm, sprinkle with the salt and sugar and 'fluff' them until cool. Set aside the saucepan with the oil to cook the kipfler chips.

Rinse the kipfler slices in cold water to remove the starch and drain well on paper towel. Bring the oil in the saucepan used to fry the shallots to 120°C. Deep-fry the potato slices until an even golden colour. Drain on paper towel.

To assemble the dish, remove the beef from the fridge and unwrap. Slice as thinly as possible (using a slicer is best, or a very sharp carving knife) and arrange evenly on a serving plate.

Using a piping bag with a small plain nozzle, pipe the aioli evenly around the plate, ensuring that there is an even ratio of aioli to beef. Sprinkle the fried shallots over the whole dish and fill any gaps with beetroot slices and herbs. Stand the kipfler chips upright in the aioli. Sprinkle over a little sumac and drizzle over a little olive oil. Serve immediately.

BRUNY ISLAND BAKED EGGS

Some of Tasmania's finest produce is grown and made on Bruny Island. It's only a small island, and a favourite holiday destination for my wife, my daughter and me, and the ingredients we love the most are ODO (one-day-old) cheese from the Bruny Island Cheese Company and the Bruny Island Smokehouse chorizo. I have incorporated these into my baked eggs recipe and believe there is nothing better in the world than waking up on a cold winter's morning and eating these delicious baked eggs in front of a roaring fire. I've experimented with many different cheeses, so if you're not lucky enough to have easy access to ODO cheese, you could use just about anything else instead — marinated feta and mozzarella work particularly well.

Shaun Groves, Tolmans Hill, Tasmania

SERVES 2

2 tablespoons olive oil, plus extra, to serve
2 garlic cloves, chopped
1 brown onion, diced
1 red chilli, chopped (optional)
1 chorizo, sliced
1 handful chopped fresh parsley (or 1 teaspoon dried parsley)
400 g tin red kidney beans, drained
400 g tin diced tomatoes
4 free-range eggs
50 g one-day-old cheese, crumbled
fresh rocket, to serve
sourdough bread, sliced and toasted, to serve

Preheat the oven to 200°C.

Heat the oil in a medium frying pan over medium heat. Add the garlic, onion and chilli, if using, and cook, stirring constantly, until the onion is translucent. Add the chorizo and cook for 2 minutes. Add the parsley and cook, stirring, for 30 seconds. Add the red kidney beans and diced tomato and reduce the heat to low. Simmer for 10 minutes, or until reduced slightly. Season with salt and pepper to taste.

Spoon the tomato mixture into 2 small ovenproof serving bowls. Carefully crack 2 eggs into each bowl and sprinkle with the crumbled one-day-old cheese.

Cook the pots in the oven for 20–25 minutes, or until the cheese has melted and the eggs are cooked to your liking. Serve with fresh rocket, a drizzle of olive oil and toasted sourdough bread.

ADAM BIELAWSKI AND ANTHEA BROWN

Poach Pear, Perth and Baillee Farm, Avon Valley, Western Australia

---

Adam Bielawski is a classically trained chef with more than 20 years' experience and a growing reputation as a master of charcuterie and artisanal food production in Western Australia. He's the co-founder of and food creator for Poach Pear, which produces handmade, restaurant-quality fine foods, including flavoursome pâtés, terrines and rillettes, which are their specialties. Being true artisanal products, they are made in small batches and no two ever look the same. 'I work with the best possible local produce available to suit my kitchen-style — rustic, wholesome and real,' Adam says.

Wheatbelt farmer Anthea Brown left a lucrative career in corporate law to pursue a passion for farming. Her paddock-to-plate philosophy means that she meticulously oversees each step of the production process until her Dorper lambs reach the customer. Her property, Baillee Farm, also runs Boer goats and cattle. Anthea spends much of her time educating consumers about how her animals are raised. 'We like to think that we're showing our animals respect … I look after them in their life and in their death they look after me, by providing me with an income and meat to sustain me,' she says.

Adam and Anthea have teamed up to create a dish for *Australia Cooks* that is a unique collaboration between farmer and chef. Their dish, Twice-cooked Dorper lamb with spelt flatbread and nut tabouli, is representative of their shared food philosophy: to create beautiful food that is grown locally, made with love and easily shared with friends and family.

The heroes of this dish — lamb, citrus, nuts and spelt flour — showcase just some of the diverse produce grown in Western Australia's Mid West and Wheatbelt regions, which also produce cereal crops, pulses, olives and olive oil, beef, pork, goat and eggs, as well as artisanal products such as cheese, honey and wine. The tabouli gives extra crunch, and the flatbread is a great way to soak up the delicious lamb juices and citrus glaze. A perfect dish to bring out at a gathering!

TWICE-COOKED DORPER LAMB WITH SPELT FLATBREAD AND NUT TABOULI

SERVES 6–8

1.5 kg leg of lamb, butterflied
1 tablespoon salt
½ teaspoon freshly ground black pepper
1 tablespoon coriander seeds, toasted
2 celery stalks, finely diced
2 garlic cloves, finely chopped
1 carrot, finely diced
1 onion, finely diced
2 fresh bay leaves
2 dried juniper berries
1 teaspoon thyme leaves
6 oranges, freshly juiced
1 litre chicken stock

NUT TABOULI
200 g couscous
4 cardamom pods, bruised
1 teaspoon lemon zest
200 ml chicken stock
2 teaspoons salt
50 g pistachios, coarsely chopped
50 g macadamias, coarsely chopped
30 g pomegranate seeds
30 g flat-leaf parsley, coarsely chopped
50 g onion, finely chopped

SPELT FLATBREAD
300 ml warm water
2 teaspoons dried yeast
2 teaspoons sugar
600 g spelt flour, plus extra, for kneading
2 teaspoons salt
4 teaspoons yoghurt
4 teaspoons ghee
1 teaspoon coriander seeds

Preheat the oven to 150°C. Season the lamb with the salt, pepper and coriander seeds. Heat a large frying pan over high heat. Add the lamb leg and seal on all sides until brown. Transfer to a large casserole dish with a lid. Add the celery, garlic, carrot and onion to the frying pan used to seal the meat and cook until golden. Transfer to the casserole dish with the lamb. Add the bay leaves, juniper berries, thyme, orange juice and chicken stock to the casserole dish. Cover with the lid and cook in the oven for 3 hours.

To make the nut tabouli, combine the couscous, cardamom pods and lemon zest in a large bowl. Bring the stock to the boil in a small saucepan, then pour over the couscous mixture and stir lightly. Cover with plastic wrap and set aside to steam for 10–15 minutes. Remove the plastic wrap and fluff the couscous mixture with a fork. Add the salt, pistachios, macadamias, pomegranate seeds, parsley and onion. Toss gently to combine, and season with salt and freshly ground black pepper to taste. Set aside.

Put the warm water in a jug, then add the yeast and sugar. Mix well and set aside for 10 minutes. Place the spelt flour in a large bowl. Add the salt, yoghurt, ghee and coriander seeds and mix lightly. Add the yeast mixture to the flour mixture and combine until it forms a sticky dough. Bring together and knead for 10–15 minutes on a lightly floured bench top. Place the dough in a clean bowl and cover with a clean tea towel. Set aside for 30 minutes in a warm place to prove. Portion the dough into 50 g balls (about 15–20) and roll out each ball roughly to about 2 mm. Set aside.

Remove the lamb from the casserole dish and set aside to cool. Strain the cooking juices into a small saucepan and cook over medium–high heat until reduced to make a glaze.

Preheat a barbecue chargrill plate or heat a griddle pan over high heat and cook the spelt flatbread for 5 minutes or until cooked through, turning a few times for even colour. Set aside and keep warm.

With the heat on high, place the lamb directly onto the grill plate or into the griddle pan. Keep moving the lamb until it is crisp on the outside, taking care not to burn it. Set the lamb aside, covered with foil, to rest for 5 minutes.

Break the lamb into large pieces and transfer to a large serving plate. Serve with the spelt flatbread, nut tabouli and glaze.

SPECIAL FAR NORTH QUEENSLAND KANGAROO DUMPLINGS

Reflecting the longstanding Asian heritages across Far North Queensland, these dumplings started as an experiment using spices, herbs and greens from our own garden. The dumplings are best cooked just before eating, although the filling can be prepared in advance and refrigerated. You'll get about 30 dumplings from a standard pack of dumpling wrappers or gyoza skins, which are available from Asian grocers and some supermarket chains.

Ellie Bock, Mena Creek, Queensland

MAKES ABOUT 30 DUMPLINGS

1 red onion, coarsely chopped
3 garlic cloves
2 cm piece fresh ginger (or 1 teaspoon ground ginger)
1 cm piece fresh galangal (or ½ teaspoon dried Laos powder)
1 cm piece fresh turmeric (or ½ teaspoon ground turmeric)
1–2 red or green chillies, chopped (optional)
1 kaffir lime leaf (optional)
1 handful tropical herbs, such as Asian basil, mint, coriander, dill and chives, coarsely chopped
2 handfuls tropical greens, such as kangkong, mustard greens, tatsoi and aibika, coarsely chopped
300 g kangaroo mince
1 packet dumpling wrappers or gyoza skins, thawed (if frozen)
peanut (or vegetable) oil for shallow-frying

OUR FAVOURITE DIPPING SAUCE
1 tablespoon fish sauce
2 teaspoons sweet chilli sauce
juice of 1 large or 2 small limes
½ teaspoon crushed garlic
pinch of sugar
¼ cup water
1 tablespoon chopped fresh coriander (optional)
1 red Thai chilli, finely sliced (optional)

Prepare the dipping sauce by combining all of the ingredients in a bowl or jug. Set aside for at least 20 minutes at room temperature to allow the flavours to develop.

To make the filling, put the onion, garlic, ginger, galangal, turmeric, chilli and kaffir lime leaf (if using) in a blender and pulse to roughly chop. Add the chopped tropical herbs and tropical greens, and blend until finely chopped. Add the kangaroo mince in batches and blend until well mixed. Transfer the filling mixture, which should be quite firm and a little moist but not too watery, to a large bowl.

Lay out a dumpling wrapper in the palm of one hand. Take a good teaspoon of filling, place in the centre of the dumpling wrapper and fold the edges together to enclose the filing. Rapidly pinch the edges together to form a pleated half-moon shape, and lightly moisten the edge with a little water to help it hold. Place the dumplings in a single layer on a large tray/s lined with baking paper.

Add enough oil in a large frying pan to lightly shallow-fry dumplings in batches, and heat until quite hot but not smoking. Place several dumplings in the pan, leaving space around each one so they don't stick together, and cook on one side until golden brown for a maximum of 2 minutes. Quickly flip over the dumplings and immediately add 30 ml water to the hot pan, then cover the pan with a lid and steam the dumplings for a further 1½ minutes. Judge the heat and decrease it slightly if required. (You'll get the hang of this the more you cook!) Remove the frying pan from the heat and transfer the cooked dumplings to a serving plate. Keep them warm in a low (100°C) oven. Repeat until all the dumplings are cooked. Serve immediately with the sauce.

SMOKED DUCK BREAST SALAD WITH BLOOD ORANGE, WALNUT AND TRUFFLE

I'm inspired by fresh produce and food markets — a symphony of tastes, aromas and colours teasing the senses all at once! This dish was created with fresh produce sourced from the Capital Region Farmers' Market in Canberra: black truffle from Tarago Truffles, smoked duck breast from Pialligo Estate, and walnuts grown by the Robertson family in the Victorian high country. Blood oranges are available at the market from Mick and Rosa Auddino, who grow them at Wamoon, and I source them from Redbelly Citrus in Griffith, too.

Liz Posmyk, Canberra, ACT

SERVES 2

2 handfuls rocket and baby spinach leaves, washed and patted dry
150 g smoked duck breast, thinly sliced
2 small blood oranges, peeled and segmented
¼ cup walnuts, lightly toasted
black truffle, to serve (see note)

DRESSING
2 tablespoons low-salt soy or tamari sauce
1 teaspoon sesame oil
2 teaspoons sugar or palm sugar syrup
2 tablespoons blood orange juice

To make the dressing, combine all the ingredients in a small bowl.

Arrange the salad leaves on serving plates, and top with the sliced duck breast, orange segments and walnuts. Drizzle the dressing over the top and shave the truffle over as a garnish just before serving.

Note: Black truffle can be found in some specialty provedores.

BRAD FYFE

Slow Food Mildura, Mildura, Victoria

Slow tomatoes, slow olives and slow pig might sound like unusual ingredients, but they form the basis of one of Brad Fyfe's favourite dishes.

Brad, who has lived in the Mildura region for over a decade, is a commercial cookery teacher at the local TAFE and the leader of Mildura's Slow Food chapter. The Slow Food movement began in the 1980s with the initial aim being to defend regional traditions, gastronomic pleasures and a slower pace of life. There are now thousands of projects involved in the movement, as well as millions of people, in more than 160 countries. Brad says the 'centuries-old traditions' that he's learnt from the community, such as family days spent bottling, tie in perfectly with slow-food principles.

'We learn from local experts and make homemade products, at the same time as learning invaluable lessons about time-honoured methods that are in danger of being lost. We ensure the continuation of these traditions and promote a strong connection to local growers,' says Brad. 'It's been a privilege to learn from the Mildura community.' Brad says that living in a food bowl like Sunraysia makes educating people about food even more important. 'It's easy to go to a supermarket and get food, and have no idea where it's come from.'

Mildura has a large Italian community with a wealth of knowledge when it comes to growing, cooking, preserving and, most importantly, celebrating food. 'I've learnt a lot from going back to the basics about simplicity … I've learnt the science behind it all, and the reason those methods are used by the locals who do it year after year.'

So what better than fresh pasta to bring these stories together? Everything that goes into Brad's dish is made from quality ingredients sourced from friends. For this recipe, Brad uses olive oil from the Slow Olive weekend, cured meat from the Slow Pig weekend and a preserved tomato sauce from the Slow Tomato weekend, as well as Woorlong Farm free-range eggs, strong flour from the Mallee and green garlic from his very own garden.

PASTA AMATRICIANA

SERVES 6

100 ml extra-virgin olive oil, plus extra, to drizzle
25 g green garlic, thinly sliced
good pinch of dried chilli seeds, pounded slightly using a mortar and pestle
1 teaspoon dried fennel seeds, pounded slightly using a mortar and pestle
300 g pancetta, sliced
sea salt flakes, to taste
500 ml fresh tomato passata
grated Parmigiano-Reggiano cheese, to serve

PASTA
400 g strong flour, plus extra, to dust
4 eggs
semolina, to dust

To make the pasta, combine the flour and eggs in a large bowl, then turn out onto a clean floured bench top. Knead well until the dough becomes smooth. Cover with plastic wrap and set aside for 30 minutes.

Cut the dough into four pieces and flatten one piece slightly. Roll the flattened dough through a pasta machine until you have long, thin sheets. Lay out on a lightly floured surface and repeat with the remaining pieces of dough. Attach the linguine cutters to the pasta machine and pass the dough sheets through. Dust the linguine strands with a little semolina and flour to prevent them from sticking together. Set aside until required.

To make the sauce, heat the olive oil in a heavy-based medium saucepan over medium–high heat. Cook the garlic for 2–3 minutes or until golden. Add the ground chilli and fennel seeds and stir through. Add the pancetta and cook, moving around carefully, until crisp. Season with sea salt. Add the tomato passata gradually, stirring to combine. Bring to a simmer and cook gently for 3 minutes. Taste and adjust the seasoning.

Bring a large saucepan of salted water to the boil. Add the fresh pasta and cook for 2 minutes or until the linguine floats to the top. Drain and add the pasta to the amatriciana sauce. Drizzle over the extra olive oil and toss through some grated reggiano. Serve immediately.

SEARED KANGAROO SALAD

Kangaroos are plentiful in the Goldfields region of Western Australia, and the taste of fresh roo is delicious. When I'm out in the desert collecting camels, we usually just barbecue kangaroo on a fire, but this salad is my favourite — the fresh flavour of the vegies combined with the earthy taste of barbecue seasoning makes this dish the way to go. I personally like to use Jamie Oliver's barbecue seasoning — I always keep a jar of it in the car — but you can use whatever barbecue seasoning you prefer.

Dan Roissetter, Kalgoorlie, Western Australia

SERVES 4

500 g kangaroo fillet
2 tablespoons soy sauce
½ tablespoon barbecue seasoning of your choice
1 tablespoon extra-virgin olive oil, plus extra, to drizzle
1 cup baby spinach leaves
4 roma tomatoes, halved
½ red capsicum, thinly sliced
½ onion, thinly sliced
1 garlic clove, finely chopped
pinch of salt
pinch of pepper
½ cup crumbled feta cheese
¼ cup finely chopped parsley, to serve

Preheat the oven to 220°C. Line a baking tray with baking paper.

Rub the kangaroo with the soy sauce and barbecue seasoning. Heat the oil in a large non-stick frying pan over medium–high heat and sear the kangaroo, browning the meat on all sides.

Transfer the kangaroo to the baking tray and cook in the preheated oven for 12 minutes. Remove from the oven and rest the meat for 20 minutes. Slice thinly.

Place the baby spinach, tomato, capsicum, onion and garlic in a large bowl. Season with the salt and pepper, and toss well to combine.

Place the salad on 4 plates, crumble over the feta and top with the kangaroo slices. Scatter over the parsley and drizzle with olive oil to serve.

CHICKEN MACADAMIA ROLLS WITH LILLY PILLY SAUCE

This recipe combines the flavours of the Fraser Coast in a succulent chicken dish — roasted home-grown macadamia nuts and basil combined with fresh homemade feta cheese, complemented by a sauce made with the berries from the lilly pilly tree in our garden.

Bailey Sheaff, Wondunna, Queensland

SERVES 2

2 chicken breast fillets, pounded until thin
2 bacon rashers
50 g basil leaves
100 g macadamia nuts, dry roasted and roughly chopped, plus extra, to serve
100 g feta cheese
olive oil, for cooking
2 cups lilly pilly berries
1 teaspoon cornflour
steamed green beans, to serve

Preheat the oven to 180°C. Line a baking tray with baking paper.

Spread the flattened chicken out on a clean bench top. Top each with a rasher of bacon and scatter over the basil leaves. Place the macadamias and feta down the centre. Roll up and secure with toothpicks.

Heat a little olive oil in a medium frying pan over medium–high heat. Cook the rolled chicken to quickly brown the outside.

Transfer the chicken to the baking tray and cook in the preheated oven for 30 minutes, or until cooked through.

Meanwhile, to make the sauce, put the lilly pilly berries in a saucepan with 1 cup water. Bring to the boil and simmer gently for about 30 minutes, or until the fruit is soft. Drain the mixture through a muslin cloth, reserving the juice.

Measure out 200 ml lilly pilly juice. Combine the cornflour with a little of the juice in a small saucepan. Gradually add the remaining juice, stirring until well combined. Bring to the boil over medium–high heat, stirring until thickened.

Cut the chicken into thick slices and arrange on serving plates. Pour over the sauce, sprinkle over the extra macadamias and serve with steamed green beans.

MATT SMITH

The Waterline Restaurant, Rosslyn Bay, Queensland

Executive chef Matt Smith says his family heritage has a lot to do with his love of experimenting with fresh local food. After his parents adopted a beautiful baby girl from Sri Lanka, Matt's mum would whip up curries to provide her with a taste of home while she adjusted to her new surroundings. 'I guess we knew from an early age how to use those kinds of ingredients and how to combine and experiment with flavours to make a dish,' he says.

Matt loves Queensland's coastal lifestyle, but it's Central Queensland's food bowl that really excites him — the volcanic soils in the area produce a multitude of fresh vegetables and citrus, while being next to the ocean provides an endless array of fresh seafood. And in Yeppoon, where reef meets beef, there are beautiful local ingredients that will inspire even the fussiest of chefs. Matt says knowing where his produce comes from, and developing relationships with other producers and growers, allows him to know exactly what's in season, and what's affecting a crop or the growth of an animal. Matt takes the business of doing their products justice very seriously; it's what drives his love of food and his passion for cooking.

From his restaurant, The Waterline, Matt's kitchen overlooks the Keppel Bay Marina and, just beyond that, the southern Great Barrier Reef. He's living the dream and says he could not imagine doing anything else. 'I don't think there's anything else that could really challenge me, or give me the instant satisfaction I get from creating something and seeing people enjoying it straight away.'

Matt's dish is all about the grass-fed beef from Banana Station, which is the family's cattle property. The beef has a more complex and earthy flavour that's often missing in more commercial grain-fed products. He's paired it with some simple Asian flavours such as red miso, Tasmanian black garlic, fried shallots and a simple ponzu sauce to enhance the earthiness and flavour of the beef.

BANANA STATION BEEF TATAKI

SERVES 4

600 g grass-fed eye fillet, cut into 4 x 150 g rectangle-shaped pieces and trimmed
4 tablespoons vegetable oil
fried shallots, for garnish
young shiso or coriander leaves
thinly sliced spring onions, for garnish

BLACK GARLIC SALSA
6 cloves black garlic, finely chopped (see notes)
2 small golden shallots, finely chopped
2 tablespoons finely chopped shiso leaves (see notes)
1 tablespoon rice vinegar
¼ cup grapeseed oil

MISO MARINADE
100 g red miso (see notes)
100 ml grapeseed oil
1 tablespoon finely grated ginger
2 garlic cloves, finely chopped

SMOKY PONZU SAUCE
150 ml light soy sauce
180 ml rice vinegar
1 teaspoon caster sugar
1 teaspoon bonito flakes (see notes)
2 tablespoons lime juice (or another citrus)

To make the miso marinade, combine all the ingredients in a medium bowl and mix well. Add the beef to the bowl and toss in the marinade to coat well. Cover and transfer to the fridge to marinate for 2–4 hours.

To make the black garlic salsa, combine all the ingredients in a small plastic bowl and season lightly with sea salt and freshly ground black pepper. Set aside.

To make the smoky ponzu sauce, heat the soy and rice vinegar in a medium saucepan over medium heat until warm, making sure not to boil. Add the sugar and stir until dissolved. Add the bonito flakes and lime juice, stir to combine and remove the saucepan from the heat. Set aside to steep the bonito flakes in the liquid for 1 hour. Strain the liquid into a glass jar, seal and refrigerate.

Fill a medium bowl with iced water, and set aside. Wipe as much marinade as possible from the beef (the miso will burn if not wiped thoroughly from the meat). Heat the vegetable oil in a medium frying pan over high heat. Sear the beef pieces one at a time in the hot pan until caramelised on each side and cooked until medium rare. Plunge the cooked meat into the iced water for 30 seconds to stop the cooking process.

Spread out 4 sheets of plastic wrap and place a piece of cooked meat on each sheet. Wrap up the meat tightly and transfer to the freezer for about 1 hour, or until just firm.

Once cooled, unwrap and slice the beef thinly. Arrange the meat in a line down the centre of 4 serving plates. Drizzle with 3–4 tablespoons of the smoky ponzu sauce. Arrange 2–3 teaspoons of the black garlic salsa over the beef and garnish with the fried shallots, shiso leaves and spring onion.

Notes: Black garlic can be found in some specialty provedores.

Shiso leaves, red miso and bonito flakes can be found in Asian grocery stores.

CHICKEN WITH BACON, PARSLEY AND VERJUS

This is a simple dish but I make it packed full of flavour courtesy of the amazing produce of the Central West. There's delicious free-range chicken from Gilgandra, tasty Trunkey bacon from Trunkey Creek, local Abilene Grove olive oil and verjus from Orange Mountain Wines. The Central West region of New South Wales is a food paradise with fresh fruit and vegetables, plus a wide variety of nuts, olive oils, wines, dairy, meat and poultry products.

Lindl Taylor, Gulgong, New South Wales

SERVES 4–6

4 free-range chicken thigh fillets, trimmed
1–2 tablespoons extra-virgin olive oil
100 g streaky bacon, proscuitto or pancetta, thinly sliced
1 large handful flat-leaf parsley, coarsely chopped
¼ cup verjus
green salad and steamed chat potatoes, to serve
melted butter, to serve

Place the chicken in a large bowl, season with sea salt and freshly ground black pepper and drizzle over a little olive oil. Toss to coat the chicken.

Place the chicken in a medium frying pan or on a barbecue plate over medium–high heat and cook for 3–5 minutes each side, until golden and cooked through. Remove from the pan, cover with foil and allow to rest while the bacon and dressing are prepared.

Use the same frying pan over medium–high heat to cook the bacon, proscuitto or pancetta until crisp. Drain on a paper towel.

Combine 1 tablespoon olive oil, the parsley and the verjus in a small bowl, and season to taste.

To serve, slice each chicken fillet into three and place on a serving dish. Drizzle over the dressing and then pile the bacon on top. Serve with a fresh green salad and steamed chat potatoes drizzled with a little melted butter.

SCOTTSDALE CARAMELISED ONION AND BEETROOT TART WITH JETSONVILLE LAMB

Our family have been farming in the rich red soils of the north-east region of Tasmania for nearly 100 years, and the current farming operation has been going for the past 60. My son Cameron Moore and his business partner Darren (Tex) Cassidy grow and market both red and brown onions, along with beetroot, carrots, swedes and parsnips. My husband and I recently retired from this business and we are now concentrating our efforts on producing the best prime lambs we can. This recipe uses three of the products we produce — red onions, beetroot and lamb.

Dinah Moore, Scottsdale, Tasmania

SERVES 8

250 g lamb mince
2 tablespoons currants
2 tablespoons slivered almonds
4 tablespoons homemade tomato sauce or paste (see note)
1 tablespoon couscous
green salad and tzatziki, to serve

PASTRY
200 g chilled unsalted butter, cubed
200 g plain flour
125 ml sour cream

CARAMELISED RED ONION AND BEETROOT
50 g unsalted butter
1 red onion, sliced
1 large beetroot, trimmed and grated
1½ tablespoons brown sugar
1 tablespoon balsamic vinegar

Note: You can use any tomato sauce — even harissa or Napoli — to suit your taste and flavour and moisten the lamb mixture.

To make the pastry, pulse the butter and flour in a food processor until the mixture resembles fine breadcrumbs. Add the sour cream and continue to pulse until the dough starts to form a ball. Wrap the dough in plastic wrap and refrigerate for 20 minutes.

Preheat the oven to 200°C.

Roll out the chilled pastry until 5 mm thick and use it to line a well-greased 13 cm x 35 cm rectangular loose-bottom flan tin. To blind bake, place baking paper over the pastry and fill with baking beads or uncooked rice. Bake for 20 minutes, then remove the baking paper and beads. Bake the pastry shell for a further 10–15 minutes, or until it is a light golden colour. Remove the pastry from the oven and allow to cool.

Meanwhile, to make the caramelised red onion and beetroot, melt the butter in a large frying pan over medium–low heat. Add the onion and beetroot and cook, stirring occasionally, for 30 minutes, or until soft. Add the sugar and vinegar, and stir and cook for a further 5 minutes, or until mixture is caramelised. Set aside to cool.

To make the filling, place the mince, currants, almonds, tomato sauce and couscous into a large bowl and mix with your hands to distribute the ingredients evenly.

Spread the lamb mixture evenly over the pastry case and top with the caramelised red onion and beetroot. Cook in the oven for 35 minutes and allow to cool in the tin for 15 minutes. Remove carefully from the tin and serve warm with a green salad and tzatziki.

IAN HAINES

Albany Farmers' Market, Albany, Western Australia

Co-founder and original owner of Kookas, an award-winning and iconic restaurant in Albany, chef Ian Haines has been deeply involved in food in the area for over 30 years. These days, Ian is the market coordinator for the Albany Farmers' Market. Founded in 2002, the market has become an institution, highlighting a consumer desire to eat local. A buzzing scene on Saturday mornings, 90 per cent of farmers travel 60 kilometres or less to bring their produce to market.

Ian himself has always bought farm-direct whenever possible. He says this not only reduces food miles, but the produce is so much better. Grown by caring farmers, it's picked for consumption (not chilled for weeks), so it's fresh, flavour-packed and the fridge life is so much longer than megastore-bought produce — and it's cheaper too!

'Know your farmer,' Ian says. 'If you care about your family, shop local, seasonal and direct from the person who grew it and then cook simply with the raw ingredients. Then there are no unknown nasty additives and you have a flavoursome meal at a sensible price.'

Ian aims all of his recipes at the working household; they're not complex or intimidating and they have a focus on simplicity. There are no bought mixes involved, and you can use whatever is readily available locally, and is fresh and seasonal.

For his Cauliflower and chicken chikka recipe, Ian uses Kojonup free-range, hormone-free chicken and yoghurt from Fairy and Co, a small dairy of Jersey cows, where the yoghurt is named for the cow that gave the milk! Vegetable farmers Howard and Bev Shapland grow magnificent cauliflowers all year round, and he gets his garlic from farmers Daniel and Simone Felton.

'I wanted to emulate chicken tikka, but in a simple manner that only involves a few fresh ingredients, and some items from the store cupboard,' he says. 'It only takes around 50 minutes to cook from start to finish. I always make my own tomato sauce from scratch, but passata or a simple pasta sauce would also work.'

CAULIFLOWER AND CHICKEN CHIKKA

SERVES 4

olive oil, for frying
750 g chicken thigh fillets, cut into large dice
1 small cauliflower, cut into small florets
1 lemon or lime, cut in half
coriander leaves, for garnish
steamed rice, to serve

MARINADE
4 tablespoons full-cream yoghurt
6 garlic cloves, crushed or finely chopped
4 tablespoons tomato sauce or passata
1 tablespoon paprika
1 teaspoon turmeric

To make the marinade, combine all the ingredients in a large bowl. Add the chicken pieces and mix to combine until well-coated. If you have the time, cover and transfer the chicken to the fridge to marinate for 1 hour. Otherwise, carry on cooking …

Preheat the oven to 180°C.

Heat a little oil in a large frying pan over medium–high heat. Shake the excess marinade off the chicken and cook the chicken in batches for 3–4 minutes, stirring frequently, until sealed and partly cooked. The sauce may separate slightly but don't worry and just keep stirring. Transfer to an ovenproof baking dish.

Place the remaining marinade in the frying pan, return to the heat and add the cauliflower. Stir the cauliflower through until well coated. Transfer the cauliflower and sauce to the baking dish and toss through the chicken. Squeeze the juice from the lemon or lime halves over the chicken mixture and place the two halves in among the chicken.

Cover the dish with foil to seal. Cook in the oven for 30 minutes or until the chicken is cooked through. Remove the foil, check the chicken is cooked and return to the oven, uncovered, for 5 minutes.

Transfer to a large serving plate, sprinkle with coriander leaves and serve with steamed rice and a fresh green garden salad.

BUNDY BEEF WITH CHILLI AND MACADAMIAS ON SWEET POTATO MASH

This recipe represents the Bundaberg region, where I live, which is Australia's largest producer of sweet potatoes and macadamias. I often buy sweet potatoes directly from the farms that I drive past and I buy macadamias from Macadamias Australia's shop at the front of their farm. Bundaberg is also a very large producer — maybe Australia's largest — of chillies (I get mine from an Asian food shop that sources them from local farms), as well as lettuce, tomatoes and capsicums. In fact, the region produces more fruit and vegetables than any other area in Australia. Beef is also widely produced on farms in the region, particularly at Gin Gin. Bundaberg is a real food bowl!

Deb Nelson, Bundaberg, Queensland

SERVES 2

¼ cup (25 g) macadamias, roughly chopped
500 g sweet potatoes, peeled and cut into chunks
2 x 150 g rib eye fillet steaks
1 tablespoon macadamia oil
1 teaspoon horseradish cream
1 tablespoon butter
1 red chilli, seeded and thinly sliced

SALAD
1 handful mixed lettuce leaves
1 small cucumber, thinly sliced
2–3 cherry tomatoes, halved
¼ red capsicum, sliced
3 sprigs flat-leaf parsley, stalks removed and leaves finely chopped
2 tablespoons macadamia oil
2 teaspoons brown sugar
2 teaspoons white wine vinegar
2 teaspoons soy sauce

Place the macadamias in a frying pan over medium–low heat, stirring continuously for 3 minutes, or until lightly roasted. Set aside to cool.

Put the sweet potato in boiling salted water in a large saucepan and cook for 20 minutes, or until tender.

To make the salad, arrange the lettuce, cucumber, tomato and capsicum on the side of two dinner plates. Sprinkle with the parsley. Whisk together the oil, sugar, vinegar and soy sauce in a jug and set aside.

Brush the macadamia oil over both sides of the steaks. Heat the grill or frying pan over high heat. Cook the steaks for 1–2 minutes each side for rare, 3–4 minutes each side for medium and 5 minutes each side for well done. Remove from the heat, cover with foil and allow to rest while you prepare the sweet potato.

Drain the sweet potato and mash well. Stir through the horseradish cream and butter, and season with salt and freshly ground black pepper.

Slice the steak thinly on the diagonal. Divide the mash between the plates and flatten to a patty shape. Top with the steak slices. Sprinkle over the chilli and macadamia nuts. Drizzle the dressing over the meat and salad. Serve immediately.

HOISIN LAMB RAMEN

The farms around our 5 acres at Canyonleigh in the Southern Highlands are perfect grazing lands for lamb and cattle. When finding a lean Burrawang grass-fed lamb backstrap at the local butcher (who is also the grazier) coincides with a classic sudden cold spell, I'm inspired to head into the kitchen to make a warming, spicy soup. This easy aromatic soup combines tender lamb backstrap with the goodness of organic buckwheat noodles, market-fresh aromatics and just-picked organic silverbeet.

Lisa Romano, Canyonleigh, New South Wales

SERVES 2

1 lamb backstrap
1 tablespoon olive oil
2–3 tablespoons hoisin sauce
½ tablespoon peanut oil
1 large garlic clove, crushed
1 tablespoon grated fresh ginger
½ long red chilli, finely chopped
3 spring onions, white ends finely sliced, green stalks shredded diagonally
500 ml fresh chicken stock
1 tablespoon soy sauce
1 scant tablespoon fish sauce
100 g organic buckwheat ramen noodles (see note)
2 cups roughly chopped silverbeet, or 2 bok choy, quartered lengthways
4 sprigs fresh mint, stems removed

Preheat the oven to 220°C. Put the lamb backstrap in a bowl, drizzle over the olive oil and sprinkle with salt and pepper. Toss to coat the meat well and place on a baking tray lined with baking paper. Cook on the centre shelf of the oven for 20 minutes, or until medium rare. Set aside to cool.

When completely cool, slice half of the backstrap thinly across the grain and place in a bowl. Gently coat the slices with hoisin sauce and set aside to marinate for 15 minutes. (Wrap the remaining lamb in foil and reserve to add to a salad, or as a filling in wraps or sandwiches.)

To prepare the soup, heat the peanut oil in a large saucepan over medium–low heat. Add the garlic, ginger, chilli and the white of the spring onions and cook gently, without browning, until fragrant and tender. Slowly add 1½ cups water, the stock, soy sauce and fish sauce. Bring to a simmer. Add the noodles, bring to the boil and add the silverbeet or bok choy. Cook for 3–4 minutes, or until the noodles are soft.

Divide the hoisin lamb slices among two deep bowls. Using tongs, add the noodles to one side of the lamb, and add the greens to the other side. Gently ladle the soup over the top, making sure to drench the lamb well in hot liquid to warm it through.

Garnish the soup with the green part of the spring onion and the mint leaves. Serve immediately. It's considered polite to slurp the noodles!

Note: Organic buckwheat ramen noodles can be found in some Asian grocery stores and health food stores.

WAYNE BRYANS

Kitchen Confidence, Bundaberg, Queensland

Chef Wayne Bryans is fiercely proud of the fact that you can grow almost anything you can imagine within his region. It is one of the reasons Wayne now calls Bundaberg in Wide Bay, Queensland his home. The English chef started his career in 1989, at The George Hotel of Stamford, a hotel with a long history — it is believed to have opened in about 947 AD. A holiday to Australia in 1994 with his now wife Susan saw them uproot and move to the other side of the world in record time. 'We came to Australia and we never left,' he says. 'We loved it so much.'

Wayne soon landed a job at one of the large international conference centres in Sydney, where he was expected to come up with 42 delicious yet reasonably simplistic dishes every week — a huge challenge, but one that Wayne enjoyed. Eventually Wayne and his family moved to Bundaberg and he has been running his cooking studio, Kitchen Confidence, since 2013. Wayne believes that when you're cooking, the emphasis should be on enjoying what you're doing; it shouldn't be a chore.

Now living in Australia's salad bowl, Wayne says working with seasonal produce is easy because the sub-tropical climate and rich red volcanic soil means there isn't much that can't be grown in Wide Bay. 'We grow an immense amount of food. I'm not sure if people are aware of how much.'

Wayne says one of the great pleasures of his job has been discovering new food producers in the region, and developing those relationships. Many of them even come to his cooking classes. 'You never know who's going to walk in the door. I now have a gentleman that walks around with trays of strawberries in winter, then there is Pat who comes in with spring onions and cherry tomatoes and there are the ladies that come in with the mangoes when they're in abundance.'

For his dish, Wayne has designed a satay sauce that includes one of the region's most famous ingredients — macadamias. Here he serves it with stir-fried local beef and crisp fresh onion, broccolini, pak choy and capsicum, though the dish could easily be adapted to include whatever vegetables are in season. Tasty, healthy and with an element of fun, this dish will be a sure-fire hit with the whole family, including the kids!

MACADAMIA SATAY BEEF WITH NOODLES AND LOCAL VEGETABLES

SERVES 4–6

2 teaspoons ground turmeric
½ teaspoon caster sugar
1 teaspoon sea salt
5 tablespoons sunflower oil
500 g beef eye fillet, trimmed and cut into thin strips
1 x 350 g packet Singapore noodles
coriander and mint leaves, for garnish

SATAY SAUCE
2 cups coconut cream
1 tablespoon red curry paste
1 handful roasted macadamias, roughly chopped
1 tablespoon brown sugar
1 tablespoon tamarind paste

STIR-FRIED VEGETABLES
1 small onion, sliced
1 capsicum, sliced
2 bulbs pak choy, sliced
1 bunch broccolini, cut into thirds
1 tablespoon fish sauce
1 tablespoon soy sauce
2 tablespoons lemon juice
2 tablespoons white sugar
5 spring onions, cut into 3 cm pieces
good pinch of white pepper

To make the satay sauce, boil the coconut cream in a medium saucepan over medium heat for 5 minutes or until reduced by half. Reduce the heat to a simmer, add the curry paste and cook out the rawness of the paste for a couple of minutes. Add the macadamias, sugar and tamarind paste and heat through. Set aside.

For the beef, whisk together the turmeric, sugar, salt and 2 tablespoons of the oil in a large bowl. Add the beef, toss to coat and set aside to marinate for 5 minutes.

Heat half of the remaining oil in a large frying pan over medium–high heat. Cook the beef for 3 minutes or to your liking (a little under-cooked is best, as the beef will continue to cook once removed from the heat). Remove the beef from the pan and set aside in a warm place.

Place the noodles in a heatproof medium bowl and cover with boiling water. Set aside for 5 minutes.

Meanwhile, heat the remaining oil in the large frying pan over medium heat. Add the onion, capsicum, pak choy and broccolini and cook for 2 minutes. Add the fish sauce, soy sauce, lemon juice, sugar, spring onion and pepper, stirring well to dissolve the sugar. Transfer to a large bowl.

Serve the noodles, satay sauce, beef, vegetables and herbs in separate bowls for the family to build their own meal.

BERKSHIRE PORK ON SUGAR CANE SKEWERS WITH VIETNAMESE SALAD

I wanted to combine Mackay veteran sugar cane with a new lesser-known local product — free-range Berkshire pork. The sugar cane and pork come from Freckle Farm, where the Berkshire pork is sustainable, chemical-free and paddock-raised. I chose to cook with the sugar cane in a less conventional way, using them as skewers, but they are great to chew when you've eaten the pork off them and enjoyed with the fresh combination of salty, sweet, sour, hot and umami flavours. You can buy the sugar cane stalks from local markets or Asian grocers.

Laura Davis, Mackay, Queensland

SERVES 6

4 stalks sugar cane
5 garlic cloves, crushed
4 cm piece fresh ginger, finely grated
1 bird's eye chilli, finely chopped
4 spring onions (white portion only, reserve green tops for salad), sliced on the diagonal
3 tablespoons fish sauce
1 small handful coriander, leaves torn
1 kg pork mince
1 tablespoon peanut oil

VIETNAMESE SALAD
250 g rice vermicelli noodles
1 carrot, julienned
1 small capsicum, julienned
1 small cucumber, quartered lengthways and sliced
¼ wombok, finely shredded
1 large handful mint, leaves torn
1 large handful coriander, leaves torn
1 cup bean sprouts
2 tablespoons crushed peanuts (optional)

NUOC CHAM DRESSING
¼ cup fish sauce
2 tablespoons rice wine vinegar
2 tablespoons lime juice
2 teaspoons caster sugar
1 bird's eye chilli, thinly sliced
1 garlic clove, finely chopped

To make the nuoc cham dressing, combine all of the ingredients with ¼ cup water in a small bowl. Set aside.

To make the Vietnamese salad, place the rice vermicelli noodles in a heatproof bowl and add boiling water to cover. Set aside for 3 minutes, or until cooked. Drain and transfer to a large bowl. Add the remaining salad ingredients and toss to combine.

For the pork skewers, cut the sugar cane into 20 cm lengths to make 12 skewers. Peel the skin using a sharp knife by pressing the blade firmly on the side of stalk and running it down the length of the cane away from you. Soak the sugar cane in a bowl of water until you are ready to cook.

Place all of the ingredients except the peanut oil in a large bowl and mix well. Divide the mixture into 12 portions and, using wet hands, wrap the pork portions around the top half of the sugar cane stalks, ensuring that the mince is spread evenly around each stalk.

Heat the peanut oil in a large non-stick frying pan over medium–low heat. Cook the skewers in batches for 2 minutes on each side, or until cooked through.

Place the skewers on a serving plate and serve with the salad and dressing on the side.

CHARGRILLED LAMB WITH GOAT'S CHEESE AND ROASTED TOMATOES

I love the idea of cooking with friends standing around the kitchen bench. This dish allows for that; it was designed to be shared and it is a perfect lazy Sunday arvo bit of fancy food. There's Erindale Farm Butchery lamb, herbs from Purtill's third-generation seedling farm and B&B Basil, garlic from Bromley Organics in Dunolly, Holy Goat 'Black Silk' Cheese from Sutton Grange Organic Farm, Pyramid Smokey Sea Salt, Saluté Oliva olive oil and semi-dried olives from Boort, baguettes from The Good Loaf Sourdough Bakery and vine-ripened tomatoes from Golden Triangle Hydroponics. Also, this platter is a great match to a Bendigo or Heathcote Shiraz. Best eaten with your hands straight from the shared platter: grab a chunk of baguette, slather on the goat's cheese, pile on the tomatoes and lamb, and drizzle over the juices.

Darren Murphy, Bendigo Wholefoods, Victoria

SERVES 6–8 AS A SHARED ENTRÉE

1 kg lamb backstrap (or cheaper cut from the leg)
½ cup olive oil, plus extra, for drizzling
1 tablespoon crushed garlic
pinch of smoked sea salt
2 baguettes
pyramid of ash-coated goat's cheese
1 large handful semi-dried olives
micro herbs, smoked sea salt and ground peppercorns, to serve

SLOW-ROASTED TOMATOES
2 tablespoons smoked paprika
2 tablespoons sugar
2 tablespoons smoked salt
2 tablespoons crushed garlic
½ cup olive oil
12 vine-ripened tomatoes

MARINADE
½ bottle shiraz (the other half is to drink!)
good pinch of dried peppercorn blend (I like green, pink, white and black), freshly ground
200 ml olive oil
½ handful of fresh herbs such as marjoram, oregano, thyme, rosemary and parsley, chopped
pinch of smoked sea salt
2 cloves garlic (or more to taste), crushed

To make the marinade, combine all the ingredients in a large bowl. Add the lamb and coat well. Cover and transfer to the fridge to marinate for at least 3 hours, preferably overnight.

To prepare the slow-roasted tomatoes, preheat the oven to 150°C. Combine the paprika, sugar, salt, garlic and olive oil in a bowl. Cut the tomatoes in half, place cut side up on a baking tray lined with baking paper and brush with the oil mixture. Cook for 3–4 hours. Keep the roasted tomatoes warm until ready to serve.

Combine the olive oil, garlic and sea salt in a small bowl. When ready to serve, slice up the baguettes and brush with the oil mixture. Chargrill on a barbecue until toasted.

Chargrill the lamb on a barbecue until medium-rare. Wrap in foil so as to avoid losing all the best juicy bits, and rest the meat. Cut the lamb into ½ cm slices.

To serve, place the goat's cheese in the middle of a large wooden chopping board, shove a knife into the centre and stack the toasted baguette slices next to it. Lay the warm slow-roasted tomatoes, lamb slices and olives around the cheese. Drizzle a little olive oil and lamb cooking juices over the lamb slices. Flick ground peppercorns and smoked salt over the lamb and scatter over the micro herbs.

RAYLEEN BROWN

Kungkas Can Cook, Alice Springs, Northern Territory

If you've ever been to Alice Springs, you might have been lucky enough to eat food cooked by Rayleen Brown. Rayleen is the co-founder and owner of Kungkas Can Cook, a catering company that specialises in native foods collected straight from country, a passion Rayleen has had all her life.

During her nomadic childhood, Rayleen lived all over the Territory, from Wave Hill to Katherine, Tennant Creek to Adelaide River. She even sheltered through Cyclone Tracy in the family bus. As a youngster, Rayleen's mum worked as a cook, so Rayleen was always helping to prepare meals for the family. Her dad was also a great chef. 'Just ask the local mob about his amazing satays. Dad hand-wrote all of his recipes up for me and I treasure them.' The family lived on bush food such as kangaroo, fish and berries. But when they moved into town, Rayleen says, the convenience of having the shops just down the road meant that they started to lose their traditional bush-tucker meals.

The chance to cook professionally came when Rayleen was asked to cater for a meeting of 100 Indigenous women in Laramba. 'The inspiration [to start a career in food] came from all of those Indigenous ladies who were so grateful for what we'd done.' It was then that she realised she could play a part in helping to pass food traditions on to the next generation. Rayleen says, 'With all of the bush-inspired recipes I make, I'll only use those ingredients that come from wild harvest to support the local women. The story for that ingredient belongs to them.' These harvest trips are a chance for the local women to commune with their ancestors, and pass along stories to their children. Rayleen says the connection of bush tucker to stories has such power; 'I don't want to see that lost.' Rayleen is thrilled that she's been able to turn her passion for bush foods into an enterprise that not only supports herself, but also the local community. 'When I talk about [the food], I know exactly where it comes from, I know the women. People want to know where it comes from, who is getting the benefits, and that it has been produced ethically.'

True to her roots, Rayleen's Kangaroo lasagne is a celebration of the native foods of the Territory, featuring a rich kangaroo mince teamed with a lemon myrtle béchamel sauce.

KANGAROO LASAGNE

SERVES 6

750 g kangaroo mince
1 large onion, coarsely chopped
2 garlic cloves, finely chopped
2 tablespoons tomato paste
100 ml red wine
500 g bush tomato chutney (see note)
melted butter, to grease
1 packet fresh lasagne sheets
250 g shredded mozzarella cheese
½ cup grated parmesan cheese
fresh herbs, for garnish

LEMON MYRTLE BÉCHAMEL SAUCE
60 g butter
⅓ cup flour
4 cups milk
½ cup grated parmesan cheese
pinch of salt
pinch of nutmeg
1 teaspoon ground lemon myrtle leaf (see note)

Heat a large saucepan over medium heat and cook the kangaroo mince, onion and garlic for 5–7 minutes or until browned. Add the tomato paste and wine, stir and cook for 5 minutes or until reduced. Add the bush tomato chutney, stir through and allow to simmer for 25 minutes, stirring occasionally.

To make the béchamel sauce, melt the butter in a medium saucepan over medium–high heat until it starts to foam. Add the flour and cook, stirring, for 1–2 minutes, or until the roux is bubbling. Remove from the heat, and slowly add the milk, whisking constantly, until the mixture is smooth. Return to the heat and cook, stirring, for 6–8 minutes, or until the sauce coats the back of a spoon. Remove from the heat and stir in the parmesan cheese, salt, nutmeg and ground lemon myrtle.

Preheat the oven to 180°C. Lightly grease the sides and bottom of an ovenproof baking dish with melted butter. Spread a little of the kangaroo sauce over the base of the baking dish and top with a layer of lasagne sheets. Spread the lemon myrtle béchamel sauce on the lasagne sheets, then top with kangaroo sauce and scatter over a little mozzarella cheese. Repeat these layers until you reach the top of the dish. Finish with lemon myrtle béchamel sauce and sprinkle parmesan cheese over the top.

Bake for 35–45 minutes or until golden on top. Remove from the oven and allow to stand for 10 minutes before serving. Garnish with fresh herbs.

Note: Bush tomato chutney and ground lemon myrtle leaf can be found in some specialty provedores, or purchased online.

BARBECUED PORK CUTLET WITH SUNSHINE SALSA

The Mary Valley is in both the Gympie and Sunshine Coast council regions. All the main ingredients in our recipe are grown in the Mary Valley except for the pork, which is sourced from Rhodavale in Lower Wonga, just north of Gympie.

Christine Buckley & Malcolm Oakley, Amamoor, Queensland

SERVES 4

4 pork cutlets
1 bunch kale, chopped and steamed for 2–3 minutes

MARINADE
1 teaspoon grated ginger
2 garlic cloves, crushed
1 teaspoon ground coriander
½ teaspoon ground paprika
2 tablespoons honey
4 tablespoons tomato ketchup
2 teaspoons worcestershire sauce

SUNSHINE SALSA
¼ pineapple, peeled, cored and chopped into small cubes
1 persimmon, chopped into small cubes
½ cup crystallised ginger, finely chopped
½ cup macadamia nuts, finely chopped
½ cup macadamia oil
juice of 4 limes
1 handful coriander leaves, roughly chopped
1 handful mint leaves, roughly chopped

To make the marinade, combine all of the ingredients in a bowl. Smother the pork cutlets with the marinade and leave in the fridge for at least 2 hours and longer if possible.

Preheat the barbecue to medium heat. Cook the pork for 6–7 minutes each side, making sure the meat seals without burning. Set aside on a warm plate covered with foil to rest.

Meanwhile, lightly sauté the pre-steamed kale on the barbecue hotplate or in a separate pan over medium heat for 2 minutes. Set aside.

To make the salsa, combine the pineapple, persimmon, ginger and macadamia nuts in a medium bowl. Add the macadamia oil and lime juice and stir to combine. Toss through the coriander and mint just before serving.

Serve each cutlet on a bed of kale with a generous spoonful of salsa. Serve the remaining salsa on the side.

SLOW-COOKED MUTTON CURRY

The Mitchell Shire region is home to exceedingly wonderful lamb, beef and pork. Mutton curry — a staple in any Indian cooking repertoire — is phenomenal. It's richer than lamb, and takes particularly well to being slow-cooked. It's an underrated cut of meat but it is slowly making a comeback. I get my mutton locally, organically farmed, harvested and butchered by The Meat Room in Kilmore East. The garlic, sourced from Blue Tongue Berries in Seymour, is also locally and organically farmed. My version of this curry is Malaysian and strongly influenced by my dad's cooking — the gravy is thick, the curry is dry and the best way to eat it is with a cold beer.

Aarathi Krishnan, Kilmore, Victoria

SERVES 4

3 tablespoons Greek-style yoghurt
1 teaspoon ground turmeric
1 tablespoon ground chilli
1 tablespoon grated fresh ginger
1.3 kg leg of lamb or mutton, boned and cut into 3 cm dice
1 tablespoon oil
1 onion, sliced
3 garlic cloves, crushed
4 large tomatoes, chopped
1 tablespoon ground cumin
2 potatoes, quartered
1 tablespoon garam masala
steamed rice and raita, to serve

Combine the yoghurt, turmeric, half of the chilli and the ginger in a small bowl. Place the mutton in a bowl and coat well with the marinade. Cover and place in the fridge to marinate overnight. (Don't skip this step, as it's what tenderises the meat and allows it to absorb the spices.)

Heat the oil in a large casserole dish over medium–high heat. Add the onion and cook, stirring, until softened. Add the garlic and tomato and cook for 2–3 minutes. Add the cumin and remaining chilli powder and cook, stirring, until aromatic.

Add the mutton to the casserole dish, along with all of the marinade. Stir well and add sea salt to taste. Decrease the heat to low, cover and let simmer for 1 hour. During this time the meat will release its juices and the curry will look very light in texture.

Stir the curry and season to taste. Add the potatoes, cover and cook for another 30 minutes, until the mutton is exceptionally tender.

Increase the heat to medium–high and add the garam masala. Move the cover off slightly and cook for 10–15 minutes, or until the gravy thickens, watching closely to make sure it doesn't burn. The gravy should be thick and cover each morsel like a winter coat.

Serve the curry with steamed rice and raita.

Note: If you like a lot of heat in your curry, you can add up to 2 tablespoons of ground chilli. Adjust to your taste.

ROAST PORK SHOULDER WITH HAZELNUT AND FIG STUFFING AND SAFFRON CIDER APPLES

My hometown of Orange is a treasure trove of marvellous produce and autumn is the season to indulge. My inspiration for this recipe comes from the agrestic, or rustic, farms there — The Farm Gate by Nashdale Fruit Co. for cream-of-the-crop apples and figs, The Perthville Pantry pork, Small Acres Cyder, hazelnuts by Fourjay Farm Hazelnuts, Goldfields honey, High Ridge Saffron, Trunkey Bacon & Pork for pancetta, Morganics Farm garlic, Paling Yards Extra Virgin Olive Oil, Mount Zero Farro and garden herbs.

Amorette Zielinski, Orange, NSW

SERVES 6

2 kg boned and rolled pork shoulder (ask your butcher to score it deeply at 1–2 cm intervals)
sea salt, to rub in for the crackling
1–2 tablespoons extra-virgin olive oil
6 cooking apples, such as Granny smith, left whole and peeled
4 tablespoons honey
660 ml apple cider
generous pinch of saffron
thyme sprigs, to garnish

STUFFING
½ cup farro (I used pearled), soaked overnight in water and drained
20 g butter
1 brown onion, finely chopped
2–3 garlic cloves, thinly sliced
4–5 slices pancetta, roughly chopped
5 fresh figs, sliced (see notes on following page)
½ cup roasted hazelnut kernels or raw hazelnuts, dry roasted and roughly chopped (see notes on following page)
1 teaspoon finely chopped rosemary
1 teaspoon finely chopped lemon thyme
1 teaspoon finely chopped sage
2 teaspoons finely chopped flat-leaf parsley

To prepare the pork skin for the crackling, place the shoulder in a colander over the sink and pour 1 litre of boiling water over the skin. Pat dry well with paper towel and rub sea salt into all the scored areas. Transfer to the fridge, uncovered, to sit overnight (or put the pork in the fridge very early in the morning of the day you are cooking).

Remove the pork from the fridge and bring to room temperature, giving the skin a bit of a massage with the olive oil and rubbing in an extra pinch or two of sea salt.

Place the apples, honey, cider and saffron in a large saucepan and set aside.

Place the farro in a sieve and rinse with cold water. Transfer the farro to a medium saucepan and add water to cover the farro by about 3 cm. Bring to the boil over high heat then reduce to low and simmer, covered, for 25–30 minutes (the farro is ready when it is tender and a little chewy). Drain the farro in a colander and transfer to a medium bowl to cool.

Preheat the oven to 240–250°C.

Place a frying pan over medium–low heat and add the butter. Once melted, add the onion, garlic and pancetta and cook until the onion is soft and translucent. Add this mixture to the cooked farro with the figs, hazelnuts and fresh herbs. Mix to combine.

Lay the pork out, skin side down, on a board and unroll it. Spread 2–3 heaped tablespoons of the stuffing mixture along the pork, making a slightly deeper incision in the middle if you want to stuff more in. Leave a 1–2 cm gap at each end, roll up the pork and tie with kitchen string. Transfer to a roasting dish lined with baking paper and place in the preheated oven. Reduce the temperature to 200°C and cook for approximately 35 minutes.

Cover the pork with foil and reduce the temperature to 150°C. Cook for 1 hour 30 minutes–1 hour 45 minutes. Remove the foil and spoon out the cooking juices, reserving them to flavour the vegetables you want to serve on the side.

Put the remaining stuffing mixture in an ovenproof dish with a lid and place in the oven with the pork to heat through. Increase the temperature to 200–210°C and cook for another 30–40 minutes, keeping a close eye on the crackling until it bubbles evenly across the top. To check that the pork is cooked through, pierce the thickest part with a knife — if the juices run clear, the pork is cooked. Remove the pork and extra stuffing from the oven. Cover the pork with foil and rest for 30 minutes.

Meanwhile, put the saucepan with the apples and cider over high heat and bring to the boil. Reduce to low and simmer, covered, for 25–30 minutes, or until the apples are soft and tender.

Transfer the pork and apples to a serving dish and pour a little of the saffron cider liquid over the top. Scatter over the thyme sprigs and serve with locally sourced vegetables and the extra stuffing on the side.

Notes: You can use dried figs but you will need to soak them in boiled water for 10 minutes and drain before chopping.

To roast raw hazelnuts, preheat the oven to 200°C. Place the hazelnuts on a baking tray lined with baking paper and roast for 10–12 minutes, turning them after 6 minutes. Rub the skins off with a tea towel.

CLAYTON DONOVAN

Presenter of Wild Kitchen, Nambucca Heads, New South Wales

'I want to educate everyone about our native bush foods,' says chef Clayton Donovan. He runs pop-up restaurants around the country and is the presenter of ABC TV's *Wild Kitchen*, so he's constantly on the move — but, for Clayton, home will always be Nambucca Heads in New South Wales.

His laidback and down-to-earth approach to cooking is driven by a passion for sustainable farming and paddock-sourced ingredients; Clayton regularly travels through the Indigenous nations visiting farms and provedores to source only the very best. For Clayton it's all about the dedicated (and sometimes crazy) food producers, their lifestyles and the landscapes they live in. He loves putting a refreshing twist on Indigenous culture and foods: think Asian-inspired water buffalo salad with Davidson plum; native flower–infused pannacotta with wild raspberries and bush honey; or spanner crab with 'roosciutto' and cauliflower purée — wow! Personally, I have a feeling that Clayton's roosciutto is about to be right up there with the Aussie meat pie.

When I first met Clayton, he gave me a glimpse of the little boy that used to hide from his mum in the 'Jaaning' tree, a tree that oozes a thick, sweet sap that Clayton would then roll onto the ends of sticks to make 'bush lollies'. He talked of going on bush walks with his aunties to forage for native foods, and learning to cook with them back in his mum's kitchen. 'I worry about our lost stories and traditions, and I'm passionate about foraging in the bush to introduce new and exciting flavours to my food.'

Clayton's Taylors Arm beef skirt with pepperberry and bush tomato rub highlights the very best of the local ingredients that surround him: native pepperberry and bush tomato, warrigal greens, aniseed myrtle and macadamia nut oil. Clayton will often pop out the back to pick wild violets to scatter over the top too. Ground native pepperberry and bush tomato, and aniseed myrtle can be found in some specialty provedores, or purchased online. If you can't find warrigal greens, you can use spinach instead.

TAYLORS ARM BEEF SKIRT WITH PEPPERBERRY AND BUSH TOMATO RUB

SERVES 2

1 teaspoon sea salt
1 teaspoon ground native pepperberry
1 teaspoon ground native bush tomato
400 g beef skirt steak, trimmed
1 tablespoon oil

WARRIGAL GREENS PURÉE
160 g warrigal greens
¼ cup macadamia nut oil

FONDANT POTATOES
150 g butter, cubed
2 desiree or maris piper potatoes, peeled and squared off at the ends
6 aniseed myrtle leaves
4 thyme sprigs
white pepper, to season
50 ml water

PUMPKIN PURÉE
1 tablespoon olive oil
½ brown onion, finely chopped
4 garlic cloves, thinly sliced
¼ cup dry white wine
2 cups diced pumpkin, in 1 cm dice
1 cup milk
100 g butter, cubed

RED CAPSICUM AND SNOW PEA SALSA
1 red capsicum, roasted and diced
½ red onion, thinly sliced
7 snow peas, thinly sliced
¼ cup finely chopped flat-leaf parsley
1 tomato, cut into quarters, deseeded and diced
1 tablespoon red wine vinegar
2 teaspoons olive oil
native sorrel and edible flowers, to serve

Combine the sea salt, pepperberry and bush tomato in a small bowl. Use the mixture to coat and rub into the meat. Cover and set aside for 30 minutes or longer.

To make the warrigal greens purée, blanch the greens for 5 seconds in boiling water and refresh in iced water. Squeeze out the excess water, chop coarsely and transfer to a blender with the macadamia oil. Blend until smooth and season to taste.

To make the fondant potatoes, spread the butter cubes over the base of a medium saucepan and place the potatoes on top. Add the aniseed myrtle and thyme, season with white pepper, pour over the water and cook over low heat for 15 minutes. Turn the potatoes and cook for a further 15 minutes or until the potatoes are brown.

To make the pumpkin purée, heat the olive oil in a medium saucepan over medium heat. Add the onions and garlic, and sweat until soft.

Deglaze the saucepan with the wine and add the pumpkin. Cook until it is almost cooked through. Add the milk and butter, cover the saucepan and cook, without allowing to boil, until the pumpkin is soft. Use a stick blender to blend the pumpkin until smooth. Season to taste.

To cook the meat, heat the oil in a heavy-based frying pan over medium heat. Fry the meat for 3–4 minutes on each side, then remove from the pan, cover with foil and allow to rest in a warm place for 10 minutes.

Combine the capsicum, red onion, snow peas, parsley and tomato in a medium bowl. Shake together the oil and vinegar in a jar and add to the salad. Toss and garnish with the native sorrel and edible flowers.

To serve, slice the meat into 2 cm-thick rounds. Spoon the warrigal greens and pumpkin purée onto a serving plate, then top with the fondant potato, meat and red capsicum and snow pea salsa.

SALTBUSH LAMB RACK WITH PISTACHIO, APRICOT, ORANGE AND SAGE CRUST

Lamb, stone fruit and citrus are quintessential elements of the Riverina food-producing region, and all three are well represented in this wonderful autumn or winter special-occasion dish. Arcadia Saltbush Lamb, produced in an ecologically sustainable manner by the Strong family at Boree Creek (between Wagga Wagga and Narrandera), boasts flavour and tenderness beyond compare. Harefield pistachios, grown near Junee, are known for their freshness and full flavour. Take a trip to Knight's Meats & Deli in Wagga Wagga for these ingredients, and visit any of the local growers' markets and backyard produce stalls for the apricots, oranges and sage, as well as greens and potato to serve steamed with this dish. And pick up a jar of Tanta Gold honey from the Narrandera Farmers' Market and some Murray River pink salt.

Amanda Strong, Boree Creek, NSW

SERVES 6–8

2 x 5–6 point frenched lamb racks (ask your butcher to do this for you)
1 cup raw pistachios, shelled, coarsely chopped
4 apricots, stones removed, coarsely chopped
zest of 1 orange
¼ cup honey
5 sage leaves, finely chopped
pinch of salt
steamed greens and potatoes, to serve

Preheat the oven to 200°C.

Place the lamb racks in a baking dish, lacing the points together so they remain upright. Cover the bone sections with foil to prevent them burning.

To make the crust, combine the pistachios, apricot, orange zest, honey, sage and salt in a small bowl. Alternatively, pulse in a food processor until they just come together.

Carefully press the crust onto the meaty area of the lamb racks.

Cook in the preheated oven for 40 minutes. Allow to rest for 10 minutes before serving with steamed greens and potatoes.

LIZ LEIGH

Caterer and food consultant, Broome, Western Australia

Liz Leigh found her passion for discovering new flavours and how to cook with them in the old pearling town of Broome in the Kimberley region of Western Australia. Within this vibrant landscape, Indigenous, Asian and European influences meld. 'I think Broome food is very tasty food; lighter, fresher — it has an Asian influence.' She was 'just passing through' 25 years ago as a Sydneysider on a holiday but, like so many Broomies, Liz got snagged and never left. 'The ocean, the sand, the pindan; it was just all of those things that grab you.'

Making a living working in cafés and restaurants has nurtured Liz's lifelong interest in food. She says even when she was front of house, she could never keep her nose out of the kitchen. After a variety of cooking jobs, Liz started her own catering business and range of spice mixes.

Using the cultural inspiration and ingredients of Broome and the Kimberley keeps Liz experimenting with new ideas and flavours. 'Our produce is fantastic. In some ways it's limited, when you see what people have access to in the cities, but I think our produce up here is fresh and good and wholesome.'

Liz has used gubinge (also known as Kakadu plum or Billygoat plum), which grows along Cable Beach, as the inspiration for her dish of Kimberley ribs with chilli-spiced salt and gubinge chutney. 'Seeing the trees fruiting in the wet season, and finding out what they were … That's part of my thing — always using what's available.'

The gubinge, cooked with star anise, brings a sharp tang to the free-range bush-beef, though if it's not available, pears or apples might also work well. Liz suggests accompanying the dish with a fresh garden salad and sautéed baby potatoes. Extra chilli-spiced salt can be sprinkled on the ribs after resting if you like that extra kick.

Liz says that combining Broome's unique ingredients and cultural mix is what keeps her passionate about food. 'It's not a gimmick; it's a true love for what's here.'

KIMBERLEY RIBS WITH CHILLI-SPICED SALT AND GUBINGE CHUTNEY

SERVES 4

2 tablespoons vegetable oil
4 beef ribs
2 tablespoons chilli-spiced salt, plus extra, to serve
garden salad and sautéed baby potatoes, to serve

GUBINGE CHUTNEY
2 cups freshly picked gubinge
1 cup white wine vinegar
1 onion, diced
2 garlic cloves, chopped
1 teaspoon finely chopped ginger
2 star anise
1 teaspoon whole coriander seeds
1 teaspoon cumin seeds
1 cinnamon stick
½ red chilli, deseeded and finely chopped
50 g palm sugar

To make the gubinge chutney, place the gubinge, half the vinegar and 1 cup water in a medium saucepan with a tight-fitting lid over medium–high heat. Bring to the boil, then reduce to a simmer and cook for 20 minutes.

Add the onion, garlic, ginger, star anise, coriander and cumin seeds, cinnamon stick, chilli and palm sugar, and the remainder of the vinegar. Bring to a gentle simmer and continue to cook, covered, for 45 minutes or until the gubinge and onion are very soft. Set aside to cool.

Put on latex gloves and find the gubinge fruit in the saucepan. Remove the seeds from the gubinge and return the flesh to the saucepan, discarding the seeds. Mash the chutney or pulse in a food processor until the desired consistency.

To cook the Kimberley ribs, preheat the barbecue hot plate or a large frying pan to medium–high heat and add the oil. Sprinkle the ribs on both sides with the chilli-spiced salt and place on the hot plate or in the pan. Cook on one side for 10 minutes, or until browned, then turn over and repeat.

Reduce the heat, cover and slow-cook the ribs for a further 15–25 minutes, until cooked as desired. Remove from the heat and rest the beef for 10 minutes.

Serve the ribs with extra chilli-spiced salt sprinkled over them and the gubinge chutney, a fresh garden salad and sautéed baby potatoes on the side.

SLOW-COOKED LAMB SHANKS WITH MAY SALAD

This is the taste of autumn — what I make when the last of the figs, tomatoes and rocket are available, when pomegranates and walnuts are in season, and when quinces are dropping off the tree. Look for these at the Riverland Farmers' Market in Berri, or swap your excess produce with a neighbour. No quantities are given for the salad — use whatever is available. There's lots of good Riverland olive oil around, including Illangi, Mitolo and Viva — I would recommend them all. I also love to use the Illalangi Caramelised Wattleseed Balsamic vinegar and Illalangi preserved lemon from Waikerie. If you like, you can also scatter the figs, pomegranate and walnuts over the top of the lamb shanks before spooning over the juices. I find that this provides a nice contrast to the sweet gaminess of the lamb.

Jenny Semmler, Glossop, South Australia

SERVES 4

2 tablespoons oil
4 lamb shanks
2 tablespoons plain flour
3 tablespoons pomegranate molasses (see note)
¼ preserved lemon, rind only (flesh scraped away), finely shredded
1–2 tablespoons quince paste, broken up

MAY SALAD
rocket leaves
fresh figs, cut lengthways
seeds of 1 pomegranate
green tomatoes, thinly sliced lengthways
walnuts, toasted briefly
½ cup extra-virgin olive oil
3 tablespoons balsamic vinegar, vin cotto or red wine vinegar
½ teaspoon seeded mustard
2 teaspoons honey

Preheat the oven to 150°C. Heat the oil in a casserole dish over medium heat.

Place the shanks and flour in a plastic bag, season with salt and pepper and shake to coat evenly. Shake off any excess flour and brown the shanks in the casserole dish for 2–3 minutes on each side. Pour in ¼ cup water. Drizzle the pomegranate molasses over the shanks, and scatter over the shredded preserved lemon and quince paste pieces.

Cover the casserole dish and seal it well. Cook in the oven for 2 hours and 45 minutes, or until the meat is tender and falling off the bone.

Place a shank and spoonfuls of the cooking juices on serving plates. Arrange the rocket, figs, pomegranate seeds, green tomato slices and walnuts beside the shanks or in a salad bowl. Shake together the oil, vinegar, mustard and honey in a screwtop jar to emulsify and drizzle over the salad ingredients.

Note: If you don't have pomegranate molasses you can substitute 3 tablespoons lime juice mixed with 1 teaspoon honey.

Something Sweet

When the local trees are bursting with fruit, don't let any of it go to waste — dip into this chapter for an indulgent treat. No matter what's in season, there's sure to be something to satisfy your sweet tooth.

When I spoke to Christine Manfield about her stunning cookbook *Dessert Divas*, Christine took me back to her childhood and her passion for the ever popular 'Passionfruit Split', an ice cream that is sadly now extinct. Her 'I go to Rio' dessert, on the other hand, with flavours of caramelised pineapple, rum, coconut, passionfruit, banana and cardamom, had me back in front of the TV, sprawled on the floor, watching *Countdown* and eating Twisties with my best friend, wondering whether I should really admit I thought Peter Allen was cute.

Australia's master pâtissier Adriano Zumbo also draws inspiration from his childhood. He grew up in regional New South Wales and developed his sweet tooth from the unlimited supply of lollies and biscuits he would swipe from the shelves of his parents' supermarket.

It's these food memories that seem to drive our talent for reinventing the comforting flavours of our past and combining them with a sense of fun and creativity. When I asked Zumbo about the risks he took in starting to sell his whacky confectionery-as-art, he credited our nation's love of experimenting and willingness to try something new as the key ingredients to his success. Although I'm not suggesting here that Twisties ice cream should become the next dessert sensation ...

There is a smorgasbord of Aussie dessert inspiration for you in this chapter. We've got ice creams, slices, cakes, crumbles, tarts and even quandong lamingtons. Yes — quandong! These recipes bring together the many different stories of Australian life, and reflect a sense of pride in fresh, locally grown ingredients and a readiness to put a modern twist on old classics. So head out to your local growers and producers, be seduced by what's in season, and whip up something to finish off your dinner with a big sweet smile ...

SLOW-COOKED QUINCES

In the Portland/Narrawong area, we have many friends who grow lots of organic produce, such as pears, apples, plums, apricots and the wonderful quince. To my delight I am given these in generous quantities from a private organic orchard in Narrawong, which I turn into quince jam, tomato and quince jam, quince jelly, pickled quince and now my favourite — slow-cooked quinces. You'll still find this old-fashioned variety of fruit in some country gardens; I would recommend trying to find a good source as fresh quinces are sometimes hard to find in shops. Portland is also an area where fresh seafood of all types comes direct from the trawlers and crayfish fleet, making it a great place for cooks and food lovers.

Brian Herring, Portland, Victoria

SERVES 8

8 ripe quinces
1½ cups sugar
toasted flaked almonds, to scatter
double cream, to serve

Wash the 'fur' from the quince skin and remove the 'bump' from the blossom end. Place the quinces in a single layer in an electric slow cooker.

Heat the sugar and 2 cups water in a medium saucepan over medium heat until the sugar is dissolved. Pour over the quinces.

Cook for 8 hours on a low setting, turning the quinces every 2 hours, or until they are dark pink and the liquid is syrupy.

Turn the slow cooker off and allow the quinces to cool in the syrup.

Spoon a little syrup onto a serving plate and arrange the quinces on top. Scatter over the toasted almond flakes and serve with cream on the side.

CIDER AND HONEY-BAKED PEARS WITH APPLE AND BERRY COMPOTE

Autumn in Tasmania's Huon Valley is the best time to find delicious pears such as beurre bosc, ripe raspberries and blackberries, and other all-natural ingredients that make a great dessert which is both healthy and delicious! In this recipe, the pears are slowly oven-baked so they absorb the aromas of the cider and the sweetness of the leatherwood honey, emerging from the oven shining with the honey glaze. The tangy apple and berry compote, meanwhile, contrasts perfectly with the sweetness of the honey and pears. I own and manage Frank's Cider, named for my grandfather, who planted many of the trees in our orchard that we still harvest today. Our cider is made from 100 per cent tree-ripened fruit grown by sixth-generation orchardists at Franklin in the Huon Valley. Cheers!

Naomie Clark-Port, Franklin, Tasmania

SERVES 6

6 large beurre bosc pears
200 g leatherwood honey
125 g butter
200 ml apple or pear cider
ice cream, cream or custard, to serve

COMPOTE
2–3 golden delicious or Granny smith apples, each peeled, cored and cut into 6 slices
5 tablespoons leatherwood honey
250 ml apple or pear cider
50 g raspberries
50 g blackberries

Preheat the oven to 180°C.

Wash the pears (do not peel) and cut across the bottom to create a flat surface. Sit the pears on their flat bottoms in a baking dish.

Put the honey, butter and cider in a medium saucepan over medium heat. Cook, stirring constantly, for 5 minutes or until reduced slightly. Pour this liquid over the pears slowly, to coat their skins completely. The liquid should reach a depth of approximately 3 cm in the dish.

Cook in the preheated oven for 1 hour, or until the pears are tender, removing them from the oven after 30 minutes and pouring the hot liquid over the pears to enhance the flavour and glaze. Repeat this step once the pears are cooked.

To make the compote, place the apples in a medium saucepan over medium heat. Add 3 tablespoons of the honey and 150 ml of the cider and cook for 10–15 minutes.

Place the berries and the remaining cider and honey in a small saucepan over medium heat and cook gently until the berries are soft. Add to the apple compote and stir gently to combine.

Serve the pears warm with the compote and ice cream, cream or custard.

FRUIT SPLICE

The Bundaberg region and all things that grow here were the inspiration for this recipe. We mix it up to include melons and strawberries when the seasons change, and find our region is never short of fruit that adds the vibrancy of mixed colours. Our kids enjoy getting involved in the preparation of this recipe and it's a great opportunity for them to help us source the ingredients and become familiar with what each fruit looks and tastes like. I like to use low-sugar jelly as there's plenty of natural sweetness on offer.

Teneale Taylor, Bundaberg, Queensland

SERVES 8

1 packet orange jelly crystals
1 dragon fruit, peeled and diced
1 punnet blueberries
4 peaches or nectarines
1 custard apple, flesh pulled out of the skin
8 mint sprigs, for garnish

PASSIONFRUIT GRANITA
4 passionfruit
juice of 2 limes

To make the passionfruit granita, cut the passionfruit in half. Scoop out the pulp into a small plastic container. Add the lime juice to the passionfruit pulp and stir to combine. Place in the freezer for 2 hours.

Make the jelly in a medium bowl following the packet instructions. Add the dragon fruit and blueberries, stir to distribute, and refrigerate until set.

Split the peaches in half, remove the stones and trim a little flesh off the bottom of each peach half so they sit flat on a plate. Put a little custard apple flesh on top of each peach.

Once the passionfruit granita has set, use a fork and rake it to a sorbet-like consistency. Scoop out balls of granita and place on top of the peach halves. Set aside in the freezer until you are ready to serve.

Cut the jelly into 2 cm cubes and arrange on 8 small serving plates.

Serve with a peach half on a separate small plate, garnished with a sprig of mint.

MANGO ICE CREAM

So many beautiful mangoes are grown here in Marian, it's a shame to waste them. So, I freeze them to use when it is no longer mango season and to make this easy ice cream that is a nice change when people are tired of eating the mangoes fresh. In this recipe, I have used the large R2E2 mangoes, which are grown locally, but you can use any variety as long as they are nice and ripe. I think the little bit of cream makes a real difference in this recipe. There's no need to add sugar because the mango and condensed milk are sweet enough. My husband loves this tropical dessert, which I sometimes make using jackfruit, too.

Lena O'Riely, Marian, Queensland

MAKES ABOUT 1 LITRE

4 large mangoes, peeled, stones removed and sliced, or 1.2 kg frozen mangoes, sliced
395 ml sweetened condensed milk
100 ml cream

Blend the mango, condensed milk and cream in a blender or food processor for 2 minutes.

Transfer to an ice-cream machine and churn for 20–25 minutes or according to the manufacturer's instructions.

Transfer to a container and freeze for at least 12 hours before serving.

Note: This will keep in an airtight container in the freezer for up to 3 months.

PEACH ICE CREAM

There isn't much that screams 'summer' more than kids with sticky fingers and juice running down their chins from a sun-warmed peach. And fresh peaches churned into ice cream are an Aussie summer served in a cup! My peaches come courtesy of the long hot summers and frosty cold winters of the Southern Tablelands of New South Wales — it's the perfect climate for growing stone fruit, and backyard peach trees thrive. For the rest of Australia, some of the juiciest peaches are grown commercially in the picturesque orchards of the lush Araluen Valley.

Hannah Cooper, Carwoola, New South Wales

MAKES ABOUT 1 LITRE

5 peaches, peeled, stones removed, flesh roughly chopped into small chunks
1 cup caster sugar
5 large egg yolks
1¾ cups thickened cream
¾ cup light milk (2% fat, not skim)
¼ teaspoon salt

Place the peaches and half of the caster sugar in a small saucepan over medium heat. Cook, stirring frequently, for 10 minutes, or until the peaches are very soft and the juice that has been released is reduced. Set aside to cool slightly.

Purée the cooked peach and liquid in a blender. Cover and refrigerate until needed. Place the egg yolks in a medium heat-proof bowl. Whisk until the yolks are just broken up. Set aside.

Place the cream, milk, remaining caster sugar and the salt in a medium saucepan over medium–high heat. Stir to combine and cook the mixture until it reaches a bare simmer. Reduce the heat to medium.

Carefully scoop out a ladleful of the cream mixture into the egg yolks, whisking constantly. Repeat with another ladleful, whisking constantly. Pour the egg yolk mixture into the saucepan and cook over medium heat, stirring constantly, until it is thickened and coats the back of a spoon or spatula, holding a clear path when you run a figure across the spatula (this should only take 1–2 minutes of cooking).

Strain the cream mixture through a fine-meshed sieve into a clean bowl. Put the bowl into an ice bath to cool, stirring occasionally, until the cream mixture reaches room temperature (about 30 minutes). Cover and refrigerate for at least 2 hours.

Whisk the chilled peach purée into the chilled cream mixture. Transfer to an ice-cream machine and churn according to the manufacturer's instructions. Transfer the mixture to a freezer-safe container, and freeze for at least 12 hours before serving.

Note: This will keep in an airtight container in the freezer for up to 3 months.

QUEEN GARNET ICE CREAM

The Inglewood/Texas region — part of the southern Darling Downs in sunny Queensland — is becoming a growing force in the production of delectable produce. The innovative farmers of the area have been producing an exciting range of foods, including olives, poultry products, dairy products, organic lamb, superior stone fruits and grapes, and not to mention wine. This recipe combines the queen garnet plum from Inglewood and the delicious yoghurt produced by the Barambah Organics dairy near Texas. Known for its deep, firm, dark, juicy flesh and unparalleled flavour and colour, our plums make this recipe exceptional.

Fiona Goodrich, Inglewood, Queensland

SERVES 10

250 g queen garnet plums, quartered and stones removed, plus extra thinly sliced, to serve (optional)
¼ cup lime or lemon juice
300 ml natural yoghurt
300 ml thickened cream
2 tablespoons queen garnet jam (see below)

QUEEN GARNET JAM
1 kg queen garnet plums, halved and stones removed
¼–½ cup water (depending on the juiciness of the plums)
6 fine strips of lemon rind, chopped (optional) and juice of ½ lemon
750 g sugar

Note: The ice cream will keep in an airtight container in the freezer for up to 3 months. The jam will keep unopened in a cool, dry pantry for up to 1 year.

To make the jam, place the plums, water, lemon rind (if using) and juice in a large saucepan over low heat. Cover and simmer for 20 minutes, or until the plums are soft.

Add the sugar and stir until dissolved. Bring to a rapid boil, uncovered, and boil for 15–20 minutes, stirring occasionally to prevent it catching and burning, until the fruit reaches setting point — put 1 tablespoon jam on a chilled saucer and place in the fridge for a few minutes. Push your finger into the centre of the blob of jam, and if the jam remains in two separate parts, it is ready.

Pour the jam into warm, sterilised jars, leaving a 2 cm gap at the top. Seal and invert for a couple of minutes to create a vacuum.

To make the ice cream, process the plums and the lime or lemon juice in a food processor until relatively smooth. Transfer the plum purée to a medium bowl and add the yoghurt, cream and jam. Whisk to combine thoroughly.

If you have an ice-cream machine, place the ice cream in it and follow the manufacturer's instructions. If you don't have a machine, place the mixture in a shallow dish and freeze, covered with foil, for 3 hours, or until the mixture begins to freeze about 2.5 cm in from the edges. Beat with electric beaters and return to the freezer for another 2 hours. Repeat this process at least twice.

Serve the ice cream on its own or with thin slices of queen garnet plum.

ROCKY ROAD WITH PORT-SOAKED QUANDONGS

I live on Gum Creek Station, a pastoral sheep station in the Flinders Ranges that boasts a seventh-generation son. These ranges are among the oldest places on earth, and hold significant cultural and pastoral history in South Australia. However this recipe, which utilises the native quandong — one of the only fruiting native plants growing in this arid region of South Australia — is a fun take on the traditional. In my rocky road, I think the port-soaked quandongs add a tartness that works well with the dark chocolate and nuts.

Lisa McIntosh, Flinders Ranges, South Australia

MAKES 24 PIECES

½ cup dried quandongs (see notes)
1 cup port
¾ cup sugar
melted butter, to grease
380 g dark chocolate, coarsely chopped
120 g dry-roasted hazelnuts
120 g dry-roasted almonds
200 g traditional Turkish delight, chopped
500 g marshmallows, chopped
½ cup desiccated coconut, lightly toasted
200 g glacé cherries

Notes: This will keep in an airtight container in the fridge for up to 1 week.

Dried quandongs can be found at some specialty provedores, or purchased online.

To rehydrate the quandongs, put them in a small saucepan with the port over medium–high heat and bring to the boil. Reduce the heat and simmer for 2–3 minutes. Add the sugar, stir to dissolve and simmer for 5 minutes. Remove from the heat and set aside to cool, allowing the quandongs to soak up the port.

Meanwhile, grease a 18 cm x 28 cm slice tin and line the base and sides with baking paper, extending 2 cm above the edges of the tin.

Place the dark chocolate in a large microwave-safe bowl. Microwave on medium (50%), stirring with a metal spoon every 30 seconds, for 3–4 minutes, or until melted and smooth.

Drain the quandongs well and combine with the hazelnuts, almonds, Turkish delight, marshmallows, desiccated coconut and glacé cherries in a large heatproof bowl. Add the melted chocolate and mix well.

Spoon the mixture into the prepared tin and spread to cover the base, pressing down gently to make the surface level. Tap the tin on the bench to remove any air bubbles. Refrigerate for 4 hours or until firm.

Remove from the fridge 30 minutes before serving. Cut into squares with a hot knife.

CHERRY ALMOND SLICE

Everyone thinks that cherries won't grow in our hot climate — they do, just not very reliably! So we don't let any go to waste on our cherry orchard. Each year any excess is bottled and preserved for later, and this slice is a great way to use them when you need to have something made in a hurry. It's a great melt and mix one-pot beauty, and it's adaptable too — I sometimes vary it depending on what I have available. My favourite part is that you only need the one saucepan. Canned or frozen cherries work equally well.

Louise Payne, Colignan, Victoria

MAKES 12–15 SLICES

150 g butter
1 teaspoon almond essence
1½ cups plain flour
½ cup sugar
450 g bottled, canned or frozen cherries, drained, and pitted, if desired
icing sugar, to dust (optional)

TOPPING
50 g butter
¾ cup quick oats
⅓ cup sugar
⅓ cup plain flour

Preheat the oven to 160°C. Line a deep 18 cm x 27 cm tin with baking paper.

Melt the butter in a large saucepan over medium heat. Remove from the heat and add the almond essence, flour and sugar and mix well.

Place the mixture into the prepared tin and press evenly over the base. Bake for 15 minutes or until just starting to colour.

Meanwhile, use the same saucepan to make the topping. Melt the butter over medium heat, then add the oats and sugar. Add the flour and mix well. Remove from the heat and set aside.

Remove the base from the oven and arrange the cherries over the top. Sprinkle the topping evenly over the cherries and return to the oven for a further 15–20 minutes, or until the topping is just starting to colour. Cool in the tin and dust with icing sugar if desired.

Note: If you store this slice in the fridge, make sure to bring it back to room temperature prior to serving or it may be a bit hard.

QUANDONG LAMINGTONS

Quandongs grow beautifully in bush settings and require very little water, which means Broken Hill is the perfect place for them to grow wildly. We are lucky enough to have several quandong trees growing across the road from where we live — they seem to love the spot and produce fruit every year. The unique flavour of quandong provides the perfect bush tucker twist on an iconic Australian favourite, the lamington. Slightly tart but sweetly delicious with an ever-so-dreamy cream cheese topping, this little beauty is so irresistible, one is never enough. Thank goodness the billy takes a long time to boil!

Lee Robertson & Claire McCrae, Broken Hill, New South Wales

MAKES 24

melted butter or cooking spray, to grease
2 free-range eggs
¾ cup caster sugar
¾ cup milk
1 teaspoon vanilla essence
125 g butter, melted
2 cups self-raising flour, sifted
2 cups shredded coconut

JAM
¾ cup washed, seeded quandongs
¾ cup caster sugar

TOPPING
250 g cream cheese, at room temperature
100 g butter, at room temperature
½ teaspoon vanilla essence
¾ cup icing sugar

Preheat the oven to 180°C. Grease or spray two 12-hole patty cake tins.

To make the 'jam', place the quandongs, sugar and 1 cup water in a medium saucepan over medium–high heat. Bring to the boil, stirring to dissolve the sugar, then cook on medium–low for 40 minutes, or until the mixture resembles jam. Set aside.

Meanwhile, to make the cakes, beat the eggs in an electric mixer and gradually add the sugar, beating until fluffy. Add the milk in a slow stream, followed by the vanilla. Add the butter and flour alternately, until mixed. Do not overbeat. Spoon the mixture evenly into the cake tins. Bake for 10–15 minutes, or until just golden.

Allow the cakes to cool in the tins for 5 minutes, then turn out onto a wire rack to cool completely.

Meanwhile, using electric beaters or an electric mixer, beat the cream cheese, butter and vanilla essence until light and creamy. Gradually add the icing sugar, beating until the mixture becomes stiff. Spoon into a piping bag.

Warm the quandong jam in a bowl and place the coconut in a separate bowl. Roll the cooled cakes in the jam and then the coconut, and place on a tray or bench top covered with baking paper.

Pipe a little cream cheese onto the top of each lamington. Serve immediately or store in an airtight container for up to 3 days. They can also be frozen for up to 6 weeks.

BANANA AND MACADAMIA SPONGE CAKE

I'm a permaculture enthusiast and for 21 years I lived with my husband on a tiny island off the Queensland coast, where we were the sole permanent residents. By this stage, our five children (including a set of twins) had all grown up and 'flown the coop'. I grew all our own fruit and vegies, and we lived mainly from the sea: luscious crabs, oysters, prawns and, of course, fish. I'm now 84 years old and have been growing my own bananas, cumquots and lemons (as well as many other fruits and vegies) for over 30 years in three different localities in Queensland. I love using my yummy home-grown produce for this cake, which is my own recipe. I buy my raw macadamia nuts from the Noosa Farmers' Market and toast them under the grill before chopping them up.

Jose Robinson, Noosa, Queensland

SERVES 6–8

melted butter, to grease
2 teaspoons lemon juice
½ cup milk
2½ cups self-raising flour
1½ cups sugar
1 teaspoon bicarbonate of soda
½ teaspoon salt
125 g butter, at room temperature
2 ripe Cavendish bananas, mashed well, plus an extra ¾ cup mashed ripe banana
2 eggs
1 cup toasted and chopped macadamia nuts
½ cup cumquat jam
1½ cups whipped cream

Preheat the oven to 180°C. Grease two 20 cm sponge sandwich tins with melted butter and line with baking paper.

Add the lemon juice to the milk and set aside for 5 minutes, until the milk thickens.

Sift the flour into a large bowl. Add the sugar, bicarbonate of soda and salt and stir to combine. Add the butter, the 2 mashed bananas and the milk. Mix well with a wooden spoon, or use an electric mixer on the lowest speed. Add the eggs and mix for 2 more minutes. Stir in half the macadamia nuts (leave the other half for the topping).

Spoon the mixture into the prepared tins and bake for 35 minutes, or until a skewer inserted into the centre comes out clean. Leave the cakes in the tins to cool, then turn out onto wire racks.

Place one of the sponges on a serving plate. Spread with the cumquat jam then top with the extra mashed banana and half of the cream. Place the second sponge on top. Top with the remaining cream and scatter over the remaining macadamia nuts.

MEGAN GARNHAM

Clean Foods, Largs, New South Wales

Chef Megan Garnham is serious about the business of wholefoods. Over a period of six years, she established an organic backyard garden to supply her wholefood café and provedore store in Newcastle. Customers embraced the fresh foods idea. Megan says, 'Consumers were shifting dramatically towards a healthy food option and a cleaner way of eating has now emerged.'

Even in an extremely money-conscious society, she says, she has found that the customer is prepared to pay a fair price for a fair product. 'The overall aim was to bring together the consumers, food producers, cooks and people who enjoy local food.' Megan is focused on regional growth and wants to encourage local food communities to process and distribute quality food in a sustainable way. '[The business was] attracting cooks, academics and the younger generation of people who are concerned for the future of clean local foods, free from genetic modification.'

After selling the café, the next challenge for Megan was setting up a cooking school and catering business, Clean Foods, while still finding time to travel to small regional communities in the Kimberley to assist with Food Futures, a social enterprise food business providing employment and training in hospitality for Indigenous youth.

Megan's Spiced pumpkin, raw honey and ricotta no-bake cheesecake was inspired by the large amount of pumpkins grown by her organic gardener husband, Mark. 'Each season, Mark saves seeds from all our produce to sew again when the new season begins,' Megan says. Some of the pumpkins are grown from seeds that have been kept and sown for eighty years.

'Pumpkins can always be bought from the farms around the Largs region so I thought it was a great way to showcase just one of our many wonderful local products,' she says. 'Pumpkin is so versatile; I just love to use it to create all sorts of recipes, sweet and savoury.'

SPICED PUMPKIN, RAW HONEY AND RICOTTA NO-BAKE CHEESECAKE

SERVES 12

melted butter, to grease
2 cups diced pumpkin
3 tablespoons raw local honey, plus 1 tablespoon extra
1 teaspoon mixed spice
3 teaspoons gelatine powder
100 ml warm water
500 g fresh ricotta
250 ml thickened cream
crushed pistachios, freshly ground nutmeg and edible flowers, for garnish

BASE
110 g butter, melted, plus extra, to grease
1½ cups hazelnut meal (process 2 cups raw hazelnuts in a food processor until fine or use store bought)
1 cup almond meal (process 1½ cups raw almonds in a food processor until fine or use store bought)
2 tablespoons panela (see note)

Grease the base and side of a 25 cm springform cake tin with the melted butter and line the base with baking paper.

To make the base, place all the ingredients in a large bowl and mix well. Transfer to the tin and press into the base. Set aside in the fridge while you make the filling.

Put the pumpkin in a medium saucepan and cover with water. Cook over medium–high heat, adding the honey once the cooking water is hot, until the pumpkin is soft.

Drain the cooked pumpkin and purée using a stick blender. Stir through the extra honey and mixed spice and set aside to cool a little.

Combine the gelatine and warm water in a small bowl. Keep the mixture warm by sitting the bowl over a container of hot water until you are ready to use it.

Blend the fresh ricotta in a blender or food processor until smooth. Add the cream and combine. Add the puréed pumpkin and blend until combined. Add the gelatine to the mixture.

Pour the mixture over the base and smooth the top. Refrigerate for 2 hours or until set.

Scatter over the crushed pistachios, freshly ground nutmeg and edible flowers to serve.

Note: Panela (organic raw cane sugar) can be found in some health food stores.

WARM ORANGE AND ALMOND PUDDINGS WITH MASCARPONE CREAM

This dish represents the Sunraysia region of north-western Victoria and south-western New South Wales — the land of sunshine, oranges, grapes and almonds. It features local Valencia oranges and almonds, and is finished with beautiful glistening glacé orange segments to depict sunrays. And you can substitute the Valencias for navel oranges when they're in season.

Carole DeMaria, Buronga, New South Wales

SERVES 4

2 eggs, separated
80 g butter
1 cup caster sugar
½ cup self-raising flour
⅓ cup almond meal
40 g flaked almonds, toasted
zest and juice of 1 Valencia orange, plus 2 whole oranges, extra
100 ml thickened cream
100 g mascarpone
icing sugar, to dust

Preheat the oven to 150°C. Grease four 125 ml dariole moulds.

Beat the egg whites until stiff peaks form. Set aside.

Using electric beaters or an electric mixer, cream the butter and half the sugar. Beat in the egg yolks. Stir in the flour, almond meal, flaked almonds, and orange juice and zest until combined. Gently fold the egg whites into the mixture.

Divide the mixture evenly between the moulds. Place in a large baking dish and fill halfway up the side of the moulds with boiling water. Place the tray in the oven and cook the puddings for 30–40 minutes, or until a skewer inserted into the middle comes out clean.

Meanwhile, peel and segment the 2 extra oranges. Combine the remaining sugar in a small saucepan with 2 tablespoons water. Heat over medium heat, stirring, until the sugar is dissolved and the mixture comes to the boil. Add the orange segments, reduce the heat to low and leave to simmer for 2–3 minutes, or until the orange segments appear translucent. Set aside on a tray lined with baking paper.

Beat the cream until stiff peaks form. Fold in the mascarpone.

Dust the puddings with icing sugar and serve with a scoop of mascarpone cream on top, and orange segments fanned out to look like sunrays.

IRRIGATION CHERRY CRUMBLE LOAF

Invented in honour of the great produce grown in the Goulburn Valley, all made possible by amazing advancements in irrigation technology and infrastructure, my Irrigation crumble loaf uses local cherries, lemon, almonds and yoghurt. I get the most delicious cherries from a friend at Turnbull Orchards — a family-run business at Tatura — and the lemons are from the tree in my backyard. There are also thriving almond and dairy industries along the Murray River so we are spoilt for choice. This loaf is the perfect snack for the farmers when they are flat out irrigating!

Amy Fay, Echuca, Victoria

SERVES 6

125 g butter, at room temperature, plus extra melted butter, to grease
1 cup sugar
1 tablespoon finely grated lemon zest
2 eggs
1 cup self-raising flour
½ cup natural yoghurt
½ cup almond meal
1½ tablespoons lemon juice
¾ cup pitted cherries
yoghurt, whipped cream or vanilla ice cream, to serve (optional)

CRUMBLE
⅓ cup plain flour
2 tablespoons chopped almonds
2 tablespoons brown sugar
2 tablespoons rolled oats
35 g butter, at room temperature, cubed

Preheat the oven to 170°C. Grease a 23 cm x 13 cm loaf tin with melted butter.

Use electric beaters or an electric mixer to cream the butter, sugar and lemon zest until pale and fluffy. (If you don't have beaters, make use of the farmers, or would-be farmers, in your household to beat with a wooden spoon!) Add the eggs one at a time, beating well after each addition. Fold in the flour, yoghurt, almond meal and lemon juice until combined.

Spoon half the mixture into the loaf tin. Smooth the surface and scatter over half the cherries. Spoon over the remaining mixture, smooth the top and scatter over the remaining cherries.

To make the crumble, place all the ingredients in a bowl and rub in the butter until the mixture resembles coarse breadcrumbs. Scatter the crumble over the top of the loaf.

Bake for 1 hour and 15 minutes, or until a skewer inserted in the centre comes out clean. Leave the cake in the tin for about 10 minutes, or until it is cool enough to gently remove.

Serve the loaf warm on its own or with yoghurt, whipped cream or vanilla ice cream.

PRUNE, BOTRYTIS WINE AND AMARETTI CRÈME CARAMEL

The Riverina, often referred to as the food bowl of Australia, has some amazing produce, including the prunes, Botrytis Semillon wine (I like McWilliams or De Bortoli) and almonds in this recipe. In fact, 75 per cent of Australian prunes are grown in the area, and I am one of the proud 60 growers in the industry. This recipe is a take on a traditional dessert from Piemonte in Italy crossed with the classic crème caramel, and celebrates the Italian heritage of Griffith.

Ann Furner, Yenda, NSW

SERVES 8–10

100 g pitted prunes, plus extra, to serve (optional)
375 ml botrytis wine
100 g caster sugar
120 g amaretti biscuits, plus extra, to serve (optional)
500 ml milk
140 g granulated sugar
3 eggs
3 egg yolks

Soak the prunes in the wine overnight.

Drain the soaking liquid through a sieve into a small saucepan, reserving 100 ml. Set aside the prunes. Place the saucepan over medium heat and simmer until the soaking liquid has reduced by half. Set aside in a bowl for serving.

Place the caster sugar in the saucepan and cook over medium–high heat until it caramelises and is a dark caramel colour. Pour into the bottom of a 22 cm x 12 cm loaf tin. Set aside.

Place the amaretti biscuits in a blender or food processor and pulse until roughly chopped. Transfer to a bowl and set aside. Place the soaked prunes in the blender or food processor and blend to form a soft paste. Set aside.

Preheat the oven to 150°C. Heat the milk in a medium saucepan over medium heat until it just about comes to the boil. Remove from the heat.

Meanwhile, place the granulated sugar, eggs and egg yolks in a medium bowl and whisk until thick. Pour over the hot milk and continue whisking. Add the crushed amaretti biscuits, reserved 100 ml soaking liquid and blended prunes and mix well. Pour the mixture over the caramel in the loaf tin.

Place the tin in a large baking dish and fill with hot water until it reaches halfway up the sides of the tin. Cook in the preheated oven for 1 hour and 20 minutes, or until the custard has set. Let the crème caramel cool in the tin before turning it out, inverted, onto a serving plate.

Drizzle the reduced cooking liquid over the plated crème caramel. Serve warm or cold with extra amaretti biscuits and prunes, if desired.

LAVENDER HONEY CAKE WITH SEASONAL FRUIT

I am part of the Tassievore Team, a group of Tasmanians committed to growing, buying and eating locally. We run the annual Tassievore Eat Local Challenge, which began in 2012. Tasmania is an amazingly bountiful place to live. This recipe uses nearly 100 per cent Tasmanian ingredients, with fruit and honey from my urban garden. You can substitute any seasonal fruit and it is truly delicious.

Lissa Villeneuve, Hobart, Tasmania

SERVES 8

230 g butter, at room temperature, plus extra melted butter, to grease
2 tablespoons finely crushed hazelnuts, to dust
2–3 nectarines (or other seasonal fruit), stones removed, sliced
1 cup lavender honey syrup (see below), plus 1 cup extra, to pour over warm cake
4 eggs
200 g plain flour
1 teaspoon baking powder
1 teaspoon bicarbonate of soda
zest of 1 lemon
125 g semolina

LAVENDER HONEY SYRUP
1½ cups local honey
2–3 tablespoons lavender flowers

To make the lavender honey syrup, combine the honey, lavender flowers and 2 cups water in a medium saucepan over medium heat. Bring to the boil and gently simmer for at least 20 minutes.

Preheat the oven to 170°C. Grease a 20 cm x 5 cm round or 28 cm x 18 cm x 5 cm rectangular baking tin and dust with finely crushed hazelnuts. Arrange the nectarine slices over the base.

Using an electric mixer or electric beaters, beat the butter and lavender honey syrup until well combined. Add the eggs one at a time, beating well after each addition.

Combine the flour, baking powder and bicarbonate of soda in a bowl. Stir into the butter mixture. Add the lemon zest and semolina. Stir to combine.

Pour the cake batter over the fruit in the tin. Bake for 30–40 minutes, or until a skewer inserted in the centre of the cake comes out clean.

Prick the surface of the warm cake with a fork and pour the extra lavender honey syrup on top. Slice and enjoy.

NEW ENGLAND 'ROADSIDE' APPLE CRUMBLE

It's been a family tradition over the years to pick apples from the trees that grow wild along the roadsides of the New England area, and this delicious recipe is a good use for them. Although my three daughters have grown up and moved away, they still request the New England 'roadside' apple crumble whenever they come home for a visit!

Janelle McFarlane, Armidale, New South Wales

SERVES 6

125 g butter, at room temperature, plus extra melted butter, to grease
800 g apples, cored and sliced
1 teaspoon ground cinnamon
2 tablespoons brown sugar (see note), plus ½ cup, firmly packed, extra
¾ cup self-raising flour
3 tablespoons milk powder
ice cream or cream, to serve

Preheat the oven to 180°C. Grease a baking dish with melted butter.

Put the apple slices, cinnamon and the 2 tablespoons of brown sugar in a large bowl and toss to combine. Transfer the mixture to the baking dish and spread over the base.

Combine the flour, remaining brown sugar and the milk powder in a large bowl. Rub in the butter until the mixture resembles coarse breadcrumbs. Sprinkle the crumble mixture over the apples and bake in the oven for 30 minutes, until golden brown on top and cooked through. Serve with ice cream or cream.

Note: You may need to adjust the sugar quantity in the apple mixture if the apples are particularly tart, as is often the case with roadside apples.

PINEAPPLE, PEPPER AND MACADAMIA UPSIDE-DOWN CAKE

This cake evokes the extremes of tropical north Queensland — hot pepper and chilli; tart and sweet lilly pilly and pineapple; crunchy macadamia; and smooth, nostalgic vanilla. Many of the ingredients are locally sourced: Daintree Gold raw sugar; Wondaree macadamias; Ottone & Sons organic pineapples; Aussie Pepper from Silkwood; vanilla beans and extract from Broken Nose Vanilla; free-range organic eggs from Mungalli Creek; and limes and chillies from my own garden. All of which add up to making this cake a favourite with family and friends.

Fiona George, Babinda, Queensland

SERVES 8–10

140 g unsalted butter, at room temperature, plus extra melted butter, to grease
1½ cups plain flour
2½ teaspoons freshly ground black pepper
1 bird's eye chilli, chopped (optional)
½ teaspoon baking powder
½ teaspoon bicarbonate of soda
pinch of salt
1 cup raw sugar
3 eggs
1 cup sour cream
3 tablespoons lime juice
1 vanilla bean, split lengthways and seeds scraped
vanilla ice cream, to serve (optional)

GLAZE
110 g unsalted butter
1 cup raw sugar
1 teaspoon vanilla extract
1 small pineapple, peeled, cored and chopped
½ cup coarsely chopped macadamia nuts

Preheat the oven to 200°C. Grease a 22 cm springform cake tin with melted butter and line the base with baking paper.

To make the glaze, melt the butter in a small frying pan over medium–low heat. Add the sugar and cook, swirling often, for 5 minutes, or until the sugar has melted and the mixture is bubbly. Immediately pour into the cake tin. With care, because the mixture in the tin will be very hot, drizzle over the vanilla extract and swirl the mixture to evenly coat the bottom of the tin.

Arrange the pineapple and macadamias over the glaze (this will become the top of the cake).

Combine the flour, pepper, chilli (if using), baking powder, bicarbonate of soda and salt in a medium bowl and set aside.

Using an electric mixer, beat the butter and sugar for 3 minutes, or until light and fluffy. Add the eggs one at a time, beating well after each addition. Add the sour cream, lime juice and vanilla bean seeds and beat, scraping down the side and incorporating thoroughly, until smooth. Add the flour mixture and beat until just combined.

Pour the batter into the tin and smooth the top with a spatula. Bake in the preheated oven for about 1 hour, or until golden brown and a skewer inserted in the centre of the cake comes out clean.

Transfer to a rack to cool for a few minutes, and then run a sharp knife around the edge to separate the cake from the tin. Invert onto a serving plate and allow to cool completely before serving with vanilla ice cream, if you like.

HARCOURT APPLE CIDER TART WITH MEDLAR CREAM

Autumn in Central Victoria is a glorious time of year, and nearby Harcourt is a beautiful community where over 40 per cent of Victorian apples are grown. Our farm was pre-loved and nurtured by a lovely Italian couple, and one of the sixty fruit trees we inherited from them was a medlar tree. The medlar is a curious little fruit — it is even mentioned in Shakespeare's *Romeo and Juliet*. The fruit itself cannot be eaten until it has been through the bletting process, which means that the fruit is placed on straw in single layers and left to soften. I was inspired to make my own medlar liqueur and paste after reading about their unique flavour, akin to that of spicy baked apples, in Sally Wise's book *A Year in a Bottle*. If you can't find medlar paste, substitute quince paste or honey. A good Australian sticky wine, like a botrytis semillon, is a good alternative to medlar liqueur — I personally like the award-winning 2011 Gramp's Botrytis Semillon. And the great news is you can polish off the rest of the wine with the tart!

Jennifer Beachey, Kyneton, Victoria

SERVES 6

5–6 Granny smith or red apples
180 g butter
180 g brown sugar
1 cup apple cider

FRANGIPANE
175 g butter
175 g caster sugar
4 eggs
1 teaspoon vanilla bean paste
175 g almond meal

SWEET PASTRY
250 g plain flour, plus extra, to dust
125 g cold butter, cubed
50 g icing sugar, sifted
1 large egg
a splash of milk

MEDLAR CREAM
200 ml thickened cream
30 g medlar paste
1 tablespoon medlar liqueur

To make the frangipane, cream the butter and sugar using an electric mixer until it becomes light and pale. Add the eggs one at a time, beating well after each addition. Add the vanilla bean paste and beat until combined. Fold in the almond meal until just combined. Pop the mixture into the fridge while you make the pastry.

Put the flour in a large bowl and rub the butter in with your fingertips until the mixture resembles breadcrumbs. (You can use a food processor instead but be careful not to over-process.) Add the icing sugar and mix well. Add the egg and mix well. Add the milk and mix until just combined. Transfer the mixture to a floured bench top and bring together with your hands. Wrap in plastic wrap and refrigerate for 30 minutes.

Preheat the oven to 180°C. Line a 23 cm pie dish with baking paper.

Roll out the chilled pastry until it is 5 mm thick and line the pie dish with it. Crimp the edge of the pastry, place a sheet of baking paper over it then weigh it down with baking beads or uncooked rice. Bake the pastry for 15–20 minutes, or until the edges become golden. Remove from the oven and allow to cool. Reduce the heat to 160°C.

Meanwhile, peel and core the apples, and cut into 1 cm thick slices. Melt the butter in a large saucepan over medium heat. Add the sugar and cook, stirring, for 3 minutes, or until the mixture starts to caramelise. Add half the apples and cook, stirring occasionally, until they start to soften. Transfer the cooked apples to a bowl and cook the second batch. When they have softened, return the first batch to the saucepan and add the cider. Cook for 5–10 minutes until all the apples are soft. Remove the apples to the bowl and let the sauce cook for a further 2–3 minutes.

Remove the baking paper and beads from the cooled pastry case. Fill with the frangipane, spreading it evenly over the base. Spoon over the apples and drizzle over half of the sauce. Bake for 30–45 minutes, or until the frangipane is firm in the centre when tested with a skewer.

To make the medlar cream, beat the cream until firm peaks form and add the medlar paste and liqueur. Mix through gently.

Drizzle the remaining caramel sauce over the tart, and serve warm or cold with the medlar cream.

PRICKLY PEAR FRUIT CHEESECAKE

A prickly pear tree laden with fruit is quite a sight to see. In late summer you'll see the dark pink fruit, which look like elongated golf balls, sticking out from the prickly branches of trees in paddocks and along roadsides here in the Western Darling Downs. This fruit has a mild, sweetish flavour similar to watermelon, but the beautiful deep pink colour is what most appeals to me.

Lynda von Pein, Kogan, Queensland

SERVES 10

3 teaspoons gelatine powder
¼ cup boiling water
500 g cream cheese, at room temperature
¾ cup caster sugar
270 ml coconut cream
1 cup thickened cream

BASE
80 g butter, melted, plus extra, to grease
150 g plain chocolate biscuits (e.g. Choc Ripple)

TOPPING
25 prickly pear fruit (see note)
2 tablespoons caster sugar
3 teaspoons gelatine powder
¼ cup boiling water

Note: Prickly pears grow wild in central Queensland and New South Wales, and can occasionally be found at farmers' markets. Make sure to handle the fruit with care.

To make the base, grease a 23 cm springform tin lightly with melted butter and line the base with baking paper. Crush the biscuits in a food processor or using a rolling pin and place in a medium bowl. Add the melted butter and mix well. Transfer the mixture to the prepared tin and press well into the base. Place in the fridge to chill while you make the filling.

Add the gelatine to the boiling water, stir until dissolved and set aside. Using electric beaters or an electric mixer, beat the cream cheese and sugar until smooth. Add the coconut cream and cream and beat until combined. Add the gelatine mixture and beat until just combined.

Pour the mixture over the crumb base in the tin and smooth the top. Refrigerate for 2–3 hours, or until set.

Meanwhile, to make the topping, put on thick rubber gloves to prepare the prickly pear fruit and insert a long metal skewer through the fruit, from end to end. Singe the tiny hairs off each fruit over a gas flame or with a blowtorch. Still wearing the gloves, wash the fruit well under running water, and cut one end off the fruit. Squeeze the pulp out into a food processor bowl and process for just a few seconds. Then, using a sieve and spoon, separate the thick pulp from the seeds.

Heat the pulp in a small saucepan over medium–high heat. Bring to the boil and boil for 5 minutes to reduce slightly. Stir in the caster sugar and set aside to cool. Meanwhile, dissolve the gelatine in the boiling water and set aside to cool. When both mixtures are cool, add the gelatine to the pulp mixture and stir well to combine. Pour over the set filling and refrigerate for several hours before serving.

QUANDONG, APPLE AND WATTLESEED CAKE

Having grown up on a fruit block on the banks of the River Murray, fresh, seasonal, regional produce has always been the cornerstone of my cooking. Moving to Burra to start my career as a home economics teacher at the local school, I met and married my grazier husband and moved onto his family property at Mount Bryan East where I encountered very different growing conditions! Faced with a variable water supply, clay soil and a shorter growing season, I became inspired by the native bush foods on our property. While most notable for producing saltbush lamb, Mount Bryan East has a feast of naturally occurring bush foods and I am proud to feature quandongs and wattleseed in this family recipe. True to my heritage, it wouldn't be a recipe of mine without a hint of citrus, with this recipe featuring lemons from my family's fruit block.

Robyn Thomas, Burra, South Australia

SERVES UP TO 30 (DEPENDING ON THE SIZE OF SLICES!)

melted butter, to grease
3 cups self-raising flour
1 tablespoon ground wattleseed (see note)
1 egg
½ cup thickened cream
¾ cup sugar
1¼ cups milk
cream, to serve

QUANDONG MIXTURE
2 cups dried quandongs (see note)
2 apples, peeled, cored and cut into small cubes
juice of 2 lemons
1 cup sugar

TOPPING
½ cups plain flour
¼ cup sugar
30 g butter, at room temperature, cubed
½ teaspoon ground wattleseed

Note: Ground wattleseed and dried quandongs can be found at some specialty provedores, or purchased online.

To make the quandong mixture, place the quandongs, apple and 2 cups water in a medium saucepan over medium–high heat. Reduce to a simmer and cook until soft. Add the lemon juice and sugar, and stir until the liquid is absorbed by the fruit. Remove from the heat and set aside to cool slightly.

Preheat the oven to 190°C. Grease a 27 cm x 33 cm baking dish with melted butter and line with baking paper.

To make the cake, combine the flour and wattleseed in a large bowl.

In a medium bowl, beat together the egg, cream and sugar. Add the egg mixture to the flour mixture and stir to combine. Add the milk and stir to combine. Lightly fold in half the quandong mixture, reserving the other half to serve. Spoon the cake batter into the baking dish and smooth the top.

To make the topping, pulse the flour, sugar, butter and wattleseed in a food processor until just combined. Sprinkle the topping evenly over the cake mixture. Bake for 50–55 minutes, or until a skewer inserted in the centre of the cake comes out clean.

Serve with cream and the remaining quandong mixture.

BAKED LEMON TART

Read Sonia's story on page 130.

SERVES 9–12

1 cup thickened cream
100 ml milk
zest of 3 lemons
250 g sugar
6 eggs
juice of 5 lemons
baby basil leaves, edible flowers and fresh berries, for garnish

SWEET PASTRY
1 cup plain flour, plus extra, to dust
¼ cup icing sugar
90 g butter, at room temperature, diced
2–3 tablespoons milk
1 egg yolk

Note: This tart is best eaten on the day it is made, although it can last up to three days if refrigerated. (And if not eaten beforehand!)

Preheat the oven to 170°C.

To make the pastry, place the flour and icing sugar in a food processor and process to combine. Add the butter and process until the mixture resembles breadcrumbs. Add the milk and egg yolk and process until just combined. Bring the dough together and wrap in plastic wrap. Set aside to rest for 10 minutes, putting it in the fridge if it is a hot day.

Roll out the pastry on a floured bench top. Transfer to a 23 cm x 23 cm springform tin. Line the pastry base and sides with baking paper and fill with baking weights or uncooked rice. Bake for 15 minutes or until golden brown and cooked on the bottom. Remove the paper and baking weights and cook for a further 3 minutes. Set aside.

When the tart base is finished cooking, leave the oven door ajar for a minute or so to allow the excess heat to escape and reduce the temperature to 120°C.

To make the filling, combine the cream, milk, zest and sugar in a medium saucepan over medium heat. Bring to the boil, stirring until the sugar is dissolved.

Place the eggs in a large bowl and whisk lightly. Add the lemon juice and whisk to combine. Immediately pour the hot cream mixture over the egg mixture and whisk until combined, taking care not to overmix. Pass the mixture through a fine strainer into a measuring jug with a spout.

Place the tart base on a baking tray in the oven. Pour the filling mixture to come all the way to the top of the tart shell. Bake for 12–14 minutes or until the filling sets.

Remove the tart from the oven and allow to cool on a wire rack.

Transfer to the fridge and chill completely. Garnish with baby basil and edible flowers and serve in slices with fresh berries.

Acknowledgements

So many clever people have contributed to this beautiful book that it's difficult to know where to start.

The team at HarperCollins/ABC Books have been inspiring to watch as this project has come together. Brigitta Doyle, thank you for believing in *Australia Cooks* and making it a reality. Your valuable knowledge, passion and sense of humour have driven and supported me from start to finish. Rachel Dennis, your creative vision, extreme patience and empathy have been the perfect 'editor's mix' and you are a joy to work with. Designer Rebecca Buttrose and the rest of the creative team — photographer Ben Dearnley, food stylist Michelle Noerianto and food prep maestro Kerrie Ray — are the masterminds behind these beautiful pages. It is no easy task to take recipes and content submitted by so many contributors across the country and serve them up in a deliciously digestible format. Bravo.

ABC Radio management must be thanked for their determination to make *Australia Cooks* a reality. Jeremy Millar and James O'Brien kicked it all off with their enthusiasm and support, Cath Hurley moved heaven and earth to give me some time away from my real job to work on this and Anthony Rasmussen drove it all home with his eagle eye for detail and his expert advice.

Our regional and capital-city radio teams embraced the project, driving the competition that produced the winning recipes featured in this book. Presenters, rural reporters and producers all got behind us to ask their audience to define their region on a plate. Special thanks must go to our content makers across the country for the chefs' recipes featured in *Australia Cooks*. Much time was spent in regional restaurant kitchens working with the chefs to capture their food philosophies and showcase their original creations, resulting in beautiful contributions from: Karla Arnall (ABC Great Southern WA); Bill Brown (ABC South East NSW); Ben Collins (ABC Kimberly WA); Zoe Ferguson (ABC Gippsland); Peter Gunders (ABC Southern Queensland); Catherine Heuzenroeder (ABC Riverland); Kate Hill (ABC South East SA); Fred Hooper (ABC Northern Tasmania); Justin Huntsdale (ABC Illawarra); Allison Jess (ABC Goulburn Murray); Ross Kay (ABC Wide Bay); Sharon Kennedy (ABC South West WA); Sophie Malcolm (ABC Mildura Swan Hill); Damien Peck (ABC Hobart); Fiona Poole (ABC Mid North Coast); Mark Rigby (ABC Far North Queensland); Alice Roberts (ABC Capricornia); Larissa Romensky (ABC Central Victoria); Emma Sleath (ABC Alice Springs); Emilia Terzon (ABC Darwin) and Rob Virtue (ABC Newcastle).

To the many people behind the scenes who brainstormed and supported the project, I am so very grateful: Nicola Fern, Michael Coyle, Natalene Muscat, Felicity Greenland, Cath Dwyer, Helen Taylor, Matt O'Sullivan and the amazing Rae Allen. Tim Gerritsen and Marc Eiden deserve a huge hug for their valuable creative input and friendship. Ian Mannix, for always supporting, ruffling my feathers and pushing me out of my comfort zone — thank you all. And to my husband, Jon Vazquez — thank you for your unending backup throughout this journey.

Our ABC Commercial Department rarely get a mention for all they do and they should, they are splendid.

However, the main ingredients are our contributing chefs and home cooks. Just look at what you have achieved! Your passion for your regions and your local food communities are the basis of this book. I am so very proud of what we have produced together ...

ABOUT THE EDITOR

No one knows food and the people who grow it, produce it and cook it like Kelli Brett. An award-winning food journalist, she was previously host of ABC radio show 'The Main Ingredient with Kelli Brett', which won the World's Best Food and Wine Radio Program award at Le Cordon Bleu World Food Media Awards, and is currently editor of *Cuisine* magazine. A seriously good home cook, Kelli has led thousands of passionate conversations about food and wine. She has worked closely with the industry's leading chefs, wine makers, scientists, innovators, experts and eccentrics to provide food for the belly and the brain for a global print, radio, online and digital audience.

Her fascination for food began in her mum's shop, Pat's Specialty Foods, in Subiaco, Perth. Behind the counter, Kelli was developing a taste for imported cheese, gourmet chocolate, exotic coffee beans and her mum's home-made terrines and pâtés, while most of her friends were eating processed cheese and polony sandwiches. She went on to work in five-star hotel, restaurant and event management, travelling extensively and discovering along the way a deep interest in food culture, food history and the way food brings us all together — no matter where we live.

Australia Cooks is Kelli's first book, combining her vast knowledge of food, and her dedication to promoting regional food communities and eating as seasonally and locally as possible.

Index

aioli, smoked 133
almond crunch 103
Anthony, Nick 130–3
Anthony, Sonia 130–1, 264–7
apple
    and berry compote 216
    crumble, New England 'roadside' 252
    Harcourt apple cider tart with medlar cream 256
    quandong and wattleseed cake 263
asparagus in XO sauce, Gippsland 26

baked pumpkins 45
Ballarat silverbeet tart 34
banana
    and macadamia sponge cake 236
    salad 33
Banana Station beef tataki 159
barbecued oysters with grilled potatoes and samphire 81
barbecued pork cutlet with sunshine salsa 189
basil and coriander pesto 104
Battle, Lyn 95
Beachey, Jennifer 256
beef
    Bundy, with chilli and macadamias on sweet potato mash 172
    Kimberley ribs with chilli-spiced salt and gubinge chutney 206
    macadamia satay, with noodles and local vegetables 179
    tataki, Banana Station 159
    Taylors Arm skirt, with pepperberry and bush tomato rub 201
    Warialda carpaccio with black pepper, beetroot, smoked aioli, kipfler chips and fried onion 133
beer-battered popcorn marron with lemon chilli mayonnaise 73
beetroot, buckwheat and Boursan tarte tatin 62
Bega Valley brunch cheese tart 50
Berkshire pork on sugar cane skewers with Vietnamese salad 180
Bielawski, Adam 139–41
black garlic salsa 159
Bock, Ellie 143
Brown, Anthea 139–41
Brown, Rayleen 185, 186–7
Bruny Island baked eggs 134
Bryans, Wayne 176, 178–9
Buckley, Christine 189
buckwheat pikelets with Sapphire Coast sea urchin roe, creamed eggs and bottarga 91
bugs, tempura with green papaya salad and sweet chilli lemon myrtle dipping sauce 78
Bundy beef with chilli and macadamias on sweet potato mash 172
bush tomato damper rolls 19

cake
    banana and macadamia sponge 236
    lavender honey with seasonal fruit 251
    pineapple, pepper and macadamia upside-down 255
    quandong, apple and wattleseed 263
capers, crisp 122
Carruthers, Eric 117
cauliflower and chicken chikka 169
ceviche, flathead with achacha and black quinoa salad 84
cheesecake
    prickly pear fruit 260
    spiced pumpkin, raw honey and ricotta no-bake 243
cherry
    almond slice 232

crumble loaf, irrigation 247
chestnuts, sautéed 16
chicken
    cauliflower and, chikka 169
    macadamia rolls with lilly pilly sauce 155
    with bacon, parsley and verjus 160
chickpeas, Mallee smashed 28
cider and honey-baked pears with apple and berry compote 216
Clark-Port, Naomie 216
confit of octopus salad with saffron potatoes, almond crunch and salsa verde 103
Cooper, Hannah 225
coral trout, crispy, with basil and coriander pesto 104
coriander
    basil and, pesto 107
    sauce 107
crayfish, redclaw and avocado salad with dill dressing 70
creamy fennel-infused prawn, scallop and salmon 'seabreeze' 114
crème caramel, prune, botrytis wine and amaretti 248
crispy coral trout with basil and coriander pesto 104
crispy fish fillets with tamarind sauce 113
crumble, New England 'roadside' apple 252
cured Murray River cod 122
curry, slow-cooked mutton 190

damper rolls
    bush tomato 19
    wattleseed 19
Davis, Laura 180
DeMaria, Carole 244
dill dressing 70
Donovan, Clayton 198, 200–1
dressing

dill 70
nam jim 78
nuoc cham 180
see also sauce
duck breast salad, smoked, with blood orange, walnut and truffle 144
dumplings, special Far North Queensland kangaroo 143

eggs
   Bruny Island baked 134
   creamed 91
   seafood omelette 108

Fay, Amy 247
Ferguson, Marianne 28
Fidler, Terry 100, 102–3
fish
   crispy coral trout with basil and coriander pesto 104
   crispy fillets with tamarind sauce 113
   cured Murray River cod 122
   flathead ceviche with achacha and black quinoa salad 84
   honey 95
   see also seafood
Fisher, Tanya 42
flatbread, spelt 140
flathead ceviche with achacha and black quinoa salad 84
Flynn, Jean 34
foraged shellfish in creamy cider sauce 98
frangipane 256
from the garden 49
fruit splice 219
Furner, Anne 248
Fyfe, Brad 146, 148–9
Fysh, Judy 70

Garnham, Megan 240–3

George, Fiona 255
Gippsland asparagus in XO sauce 26
Gold Coast surf 'n' surf 117
Goodisson, Wendy 50
Goodrich, Fiona 228
granita, passionfruit 219
grape pickle, sun muscat 20
green papaya salad 78
grilled Tassie oysters with smoked salmon and camembert 69
Groves, Shaun 134
gubinge chutney 206

Haines, Ian 166, 168–9
Hasell, Dee 69
Herring, Brian 215
Hickson, Annabelle 45
Hill, Helen 84
Hinds, Amanda 108
hoisin lamb ramen 175
honey fish 95
horseradish cream 122
Hudson, Roslyn 20

ice cream
   mango 222
   peach 225
   Queen Garnet 228

Jones, Huw 88–91

kangaroo
   dumplings, special Far North Queensland 143
   lasagne 186
   seared, salad 150
Kent, Peter 120–3
Kimberley ribs with chilli-spiced salt and gubinge chutney 206
kipfler chips 133
Krishnan, Aarathi 190

lamb
   chargrilled, with goat's cheese and roasted tomatoes 183
   hoisin ramen 175
   saltbush rack with pistachio, orange and sage crust 202
   Scottsdale caramelised onion and beetroot tart with Jetsonville lamb 165
   slow-cooked shanks with May salad 209
   twice-cooked Dorper, with spelt flatbread and nut tabouli 140
lavender honey
   cake with seasonal fruit 251
   syrup 251
Leach, Andy 92
Leigh, Liz 205–7
lemon myrtle
   béchamel sauce 186
   brioche crumbs 122
lemon tart, baked 264
Lewis, Chris 98
loaf, irrigation cherry crumble 247
Lupin, Emma 37–9
lupin pancakes, vegetarian savoury 41

macadamia
   banana and, sponge cake 236
   satay beef with noodles and local vegetables 179
   Bundy beef with chilli and, on sweet potato mash 172
   chicken rolls with lilly pilly sauce 155
   pineapple, pepper and, upside-down cake 255
   satay beef with noodles and local vegetables 179
McCrae, Claire 235
McFarlane, Janelle 252
MacIntosh, Lisa 231
Mallee smashed chickpeas 28

mango ice cream 222
Marchwicki, Noelene 114
Maroochy River mud crab cakes 92
marron, beer-battered popcorn with lemon chilli mayonnaise 73
May salad 209
mayonnaise, wasabi 103
medlar cream 256
miso marinade 159
Moore, Dinah 165
mud crab cakes, Maroochy River 92
Murphy, Darren 183
Murray River cod
   cured 122
   wattleseed and bush pepper, with tomato and coriander sauces 107
mutton curry, slow-cooked 190

nam jim dressing 78
Nelson, Deb 172
nuoc cham dressing 180
nut tabouli 140

Oakley, Malcolm 189
octopus salad, confit of, with saffron potatoes, almond crunch and salsa verde 103
omelette, seafood 108
onions, caramelised red and beetroot 165
orange
   gel 122
   vinaigrette 122
   warm orange and almond puddings with mascarpone cream 244
O'Riely, Lena 222
oysters
   barbecued with grilled potatoes and samphire 81
   grilled Tassie with smoked salmon and camembert 69

pancakes, vegetarian savoury lupin 41
passionfruit granita 219
pasta 149
   amatriciana 149
   kangaroo lasagne 186
   tortellini, pumpkin and ash chevre, with citrus beurre noisette 56
pastry 165
   sweet 256, 264
Payne, Louise 232
peach ice cream 225
pears, cider and honey-baked with apple and berry compote 216
pesto, basil and coriander 104
pickle, sun muscat grape 20
pies, roasted vegetable and feta 42
pikelets, buckwheat 91
pineapple
   mango salsa 117
   pepper and macadamia upside-down cake 255
plum
   jam 228
   Queen Garnet ice cream 228
ponzu sauce, smoky 159
pork
   barbecued cutlet with sunshine salsa 189
   Berkshire, on sugar cane skewers with Vietnamese salad 180
   roast shoulder with hazelnut and fig stuffing and saffron cider apples 195–6
potatoes
   fondant 201
   kipfler chips 133
   saffron 103
Pozmyk, Liz 144
prawn, scallop and salmon 'seabreeze', creamy fennel-infused 114
prickly pear fruit cheesecake 260
Prince, Lewis 25–7
prune, botrytis wine and amaretti crème caramel 248
puddings, warm orange and almond with mascarpone cream 244
pumpkin
   and ash chevre tortellini with citrus beurre noisette 56
   baked 45
   purée 201
   spiced, raw honey and ricotta no-bake cheesecake 243

quandong
   apple and wattleseed cake 263
   lamingtons 235
   rocky road with port-soaked 231
Queen Garnet ice cream 228
quinces, slow-cooked 215
Quinn, Noelle 110, 112–13

ramen, hoisin lamb 175
ratatouille, upside-down 55
red capsicum and snow pea salsa 201
redclaw crayfish and avocado salad with dill dressing 70
roast pork shoulder with hazelnut and fig stuffing and saffron cider apples 195–6
roasted rainbow salad of green paw paw and Top End dry-season garden produce 38
roasted vegetable and feta pies 42
Robertson, Lee 235
Robinson, Jose 236
rocky road with port-soaked quandongs 231
Roissetter, Dan 150
Romano, Lisa 175
Rose-Jones, Murray 73
rub, saltbush 15

saffron potatoes 103
salad 172
   confit of octopus, with saffron potatoes, almond crunch and salsa verde 103
   green papaya 78
   May 209
   redclaw crayfish and avocado, with dill dressing 70
   roasted rainbow salad of green paw paw and Top End dry-season garden produce 38
   seared kangaroo 150

smoked duck breast, with blood orange, walnut and truffle 144
Vietnamese 180
salsa
   black garlic 159
   pineapple mango 117
   red capsicum and snow pea 201
   sunshine 189
   verde 103
saltbush
   lamb rack with pistachio, orange and sage crust 202
   rub 15
satay sauce 179
sauces
   coriander 107
   lemon myrtle béchamel 186
   satay 179
   tamarind 113
   tomato 107
   see also dressing
Scottsdale caramelised onion and beetroot tart with Jetsonville lamb 165
seafood
   buckwheat pikelets with Sapphire Coast sea urchin roe, creamed eggs and bottarga 91
   bugs, tempura with green papaya salad and sweet chilli lemon myrtle dipping sauce 78
   coral trout, crispy with basil and coriander pesto 104
   crayfish, redclaw and avocado salad with dill dressing 70
   fish fillets, crispy with tamarind sauce 113
   flathead ceviche with achacha and black quinoa salad 84
   honey fish 95
   marron, beer-battered popcorn with lemon chilli mayonnaise 73
   mud crab cakes, Maroochy River 92
   Murray cod, wattleseed and bush pepper with tomato and coriander sauces 107

octopus salad, confit of, with saffron potatoes, almond crunch and salsa verde 103
omelette 108
oysters, barbecued with grilled potatoes and samphire 81
oysters, grilled Tassie with smoked salmon and camembert 69
prawn, scallop and salmon 'seabreeze', creamy fennel-infused 114
shellfish, foraged, in creamy cider sauce 98
surf 'n' surf, Gold Coast 117
seared kangaroo salad 150
Sheaff, Bailey 155
Shearing, Kirby 46, 48–9
shellfish, foraged, in creamy cider sauce 98
silverbeet tart, Ballarat 34
Simms, Joan 16, 107
slice, cherry almond 232
slow-cooked lamb shanks with May salad 209
slow-roasted tomatoes 183
Smith, Matt 156, 158–9
smoked duck breast salad with blood orange, walnut and truffle 144
spelt flatbread 140
Squire, Craig 77–9
Strong, Amanda 202
surf 'n' surf, Gold Coast 117
Szeremeta, Kylie 56

tabouli, nut 140
tamarind sauce 113
tarte tatin, beetroot, buckwheat and Boursan 62
tarts
   baked lemon 264
   Ballarat silverbeet 34
   Bega Valley brunch cheese 50
   Harcourt apple cider, with medlar cream 256
   Scottsdale caramelised onion and beetroot, with Jetsonville lamb 165
Taylor, Lindl 160

Taylor, Teneale 219
Taylors Arm beef skirt, with pepperberry and bush tomato rub 201
tempura bugs with green papaya salad and sweet chilli lemon myrtle dipping sauce 78
tomato
   sauce 107
   slow-roasted 183
tortellini, pumpkin and ash chevre with citrus beurre noisette 56
Tourenq, Christophe 55
Tourenq, Debra 55
Tschirner, Andrea 15
twice-cooked Dorper lamb with spelt flatbread and nut tabouli 140

upside-down ratatouille 55

vegetables, stir-fried 179
Vietnamese salad 180
Villeneuve, Lissa 251
Vishnumohan, Dr Shyamala 41
von Pein, Lynda 260

Warialda beef carpaccio with black pepper, beetroot, smoked aioli, kipfler chips and fried onion 133
Wark, Athol 19
Warrigal greens purée 201
wasabi mayonnaise 103
wattleseed
   and bush pepper Murray cod with tomato and coriander sauces 107
   damper rolls 19
   quandong, apple and, cake 263
Whitelaw, Stuart 81
Williams, Chris 33
Winfield, Niccole 104

Zalokar, Sophie 61–3
Zielinski, Amorette 195

Picture credits

Page 27 by Zoe Ferguson; page 39 (top left and bottom) by Emilia Terzon; page 39 (top right) by Emma Lupin; page 48 by Kate Hill; page 63 (top left and bottom) by Sharon Kennedy; page 79 (top and bottom right) by Mark Rigby; page 79 (bottom left) courtesy of Craig Squire; page 90 by Bill Brown; page 101 by Auscape/UIG/Getty Images; page 102 by Fred Hooper; page 111 by John Clark Photo/Getty Images; page 112 by Allison Jess; page 120 by Daniel Schmidt; page 123 (top left, bottom right) by Daniel Schmidt; page 123 (top right, bottom left) by Catherine Heuzenroeder; page 131–2 and 265 by Larissa Romensky; page 138, 141 (bottom right) and 168 by Karla Arnall; page 141 (top left) by Crib Creative/PRIMOLife Magazine; page 141 (top right) by Marissa Bielawski; page 141 (bottom left) by Nectarine Photography; page 148 by Sophie Malcolm; page 157 by Australian Scenics/Getty Images; page 158 by Alice Roberts; page 167 by Jamie Marshall – Tribaleye Images/Getty Images; page 178 by Ross Kay; page 187 by Emma Sleath; page 199 by Manfred Gottschalk/Getty Images; page 200 by Russell Pell; page 207 by Ben Collins and page 241–2 by Rob Virtue.

The images on the following pages by shutterstock.com: 22–3 (Lamington National Park, Queensland), 24, 36, 47, 58–9 (McLaren Vale, South Australia), 67, 76, 82–3 (Great Ocean Road, Victoria), 89, 118–9 (Byron Bay, New South Wales), 128–9, 138, 147, 152–3 (Yelverton, Western Australia), 162–3 (Grampians National Park, Victoria), 169, 177, 184, 192–3 (Rawdon Vale, New South Wales), 197, 204, 226–7, 238–9 (Gawler, South Australia).

All other images by Ben Dearnley.

 The ABC 'Wave' device is a trademark of the Australian Broadcasting Corporation and is used under licence by HarperCollinsPublishers Australia.

First published in 2016
by HarperCollins*Publishers* Australia Pty Limited
ABN 36 009 913 517
harpercollins.com.au

Compilation copyright © Australian Broadcasting Corporation 2016

This work is copyright. Apart from any use as permitted under the *Copyright Act 1968*, no part may be reproduced, copied, scanned, stored in a retrieval system, recorded, or transmitted, in any form or by any means, without the prior written permission of the publisher.

HarperCollins*Publishers*
Level 13, 201 Elizabeth Street, Sydney, NSW 2000, Australia
Unit D1, 63 Apollo Drive, Rosedale, Auckland 0632, New Zealand
A 53, Sector 57, Noida, UP, India
1 London Bridge Street, London, SE1 9GF, United Kingdom
2 Bloor Street East, 20th floor, Toronto, Ontario M4W 1A8, Canada
195 Broadway, New York, NY 10007, USA

National Library of Australia
Cataloguing-in-Publication data:

Australia cooks / edited by Kelli Brett.
   978 0 7333 3461 0 (hardback)
   Includes index.
   Cooking, Australian.
   Food habits — Australia.
   Cookbooks.
   Australia — Social life and customs.
   Brett, Kelli, editor.
641.5994

Cover design by HarperCollins Design Studio and Rebecca Buttrose
Front cover image by Ben Dearnley
Back cover image by shutterstock.com
Internal design and layout by Rebecca Buttrose
Food styling by Michelle Noerianto
Food preparation by Kerrie Ray
Ceramics on pages 10, 11 and 13 by Jo Norton, Thrown by Jo
Colour reproduction by Graphic Print Group, Adelaide
Printed and bound in China by RR Donnelley

5 4 3 2 1   16 17 18 19